LEADING
BY LISTENING
& OBEYING

LEADING
BY LISTENING
& OBEYING

Building Great Teams Starts with YOU!

JASON T. QUIMBY

ARPress

ILLUMINATING IDEAS.
EMPOWERING VOICES

ARPress
45 Dan Road Suite 5
Canton MA 02021

Hotline: 1(888) 821-0229
Fax: 1(508) 545-7580

Ordering Information:
Quantity sales. Special discounts are available on quantity purchases by corporations, associations, and others. For details, contact the publisher at the address above.

Printed in the United States of America.

ISBN-13:   Softcover   979-8-88514-105-5
              eBook   979-8-88514-104-8

Library of Congress Control Number: 2021924494

Table Of Contents

Author's Note

There is an African proverb that states:
"If you want to go fast, go alone. If you want to go far, go together."

"Going together" captures the essence of what great teambuilding is about. The point is NOT to only have more people to share the journey with. The point is to have a group of people that can work in unison to achieve a common mission.

The following pages capture experiences that were recorded in 2014 just after I completed my 20-year career at Iberia Tiles. As President/CEO, I had just facilitated the sale of Iberia Tiles Corporation to a new ownership group. After this sale, I was fortunate to be soon after, in a position to take my first sabbatical and capture the experiences and lessons of the previous 20 years.

Little did I know that from 2016-2017 I would be taking a second sabbatical which was "forced" by my wife's diagnosis of Acute Lymphoblastic Leukemia with a very grim 5year plus prognosis. I am happy to say that now, after 5 years she is cancer free and thriving. This celebration does not come without a great deal of monetary, emotional, and physical sacrifice. Our family could not have achieved this recovery without God's grace via prayer and support from a great amount of people which also supports the African proverb which I reference above, "If you want to go far, go together." We had a "village" of over 200 prayer warriors and friends who donated time, talent, and treasure to help keep our family thriving during the 180 days that in 2016 my wife spent in the hospital as well as the 5 years of post-treatment recovery. We will never be able to express the gratitude that we have in our hearts for each one of you.

From 1994 to 2016, my wife and I lived in Miami where we raised our three daughters. Shortly after my wife's diagnosis we moved the family to NYC for her to be treated at the famous Memorial Sloan Kettering Cancer Center. We spent a year in NYC which was a huge transition for my middle school and high-school aged daughters. They are now young adults transitioning from High School to College and also thriving. During my time in NYC I continued to operate 3 businesses that I started in 2015: QM Resources Consulting, Marina & Carrara Mediterranean Swim Lifestyle, and TiLE Gallery by Marmol. I was very fortunate to have tremendous clients and partners that helped make my remote contributions possible. Shortly prior to this time I met one of my most treasured clients in John Faour and Angelo Rivera at Faour Glass Technologies with whom until this day, I am spending many hours perfecting the art of building great teams for the benefit of SLIMPACT! Follow my Instagram page @qmresources to learn more about SLIMPACT.

During my time in New York City, I continued to write articles about my various experiences that have been captured in this introduction for the NEW EDITION of my book "Leading by Listening and Obeying, Building Great Teams Starts with You".

Building Great Teams should be an objective for every professional. Most of you will either be part of a team or leading a team and therefore everything you find in this book will be helpful on your journey.

ACKNOWLEDGEMENTS

I give thanks to God for His many blessings to me and my family. This book is the culmination of acquired knowledge and experiences over my lifetime and has been influenced by every single person that I have had the pleasure of knowing. I thank my Mom and Dad for leading by example of faithful obedience. I share my Dad's love of people and his outgoing personality, allowing us both to easily connect with others. My Mom has helped me strive for excellence in everything I do. I thank her for her educational dedication which has helped me be patient and listen to others. I thank my wife and best friend for being by my side during good times and bad. Everything I have been able to accomplish professionally has been facilitated by her support and encouragement. I thank my three beautiful daughters for defining one of life's broader purposes and helping teach me humility and patience. They have helped me realize that family is the most important thing in life. The most challenging and rewarding job I could ever hope for is being Dad.

My tutors and professors throughout my education helped develop my love for learning and striving for excellence. One of the common lessons is that history will repeat itself. All we need to do is observe and listen to the wisdom of others and learn to embrace similar experiences in the future. Bruce Reeder, Tom Hilyer, Kenny Park, Jane Burdeshaw, Eduardo Garguravich, Nick Gerogianis, and Dr. Gil Ramirez are just a few of the educators who deserve special mention in the molding of my development as a student, and later as an employee. Professionally, I thank the Alabama State Bar team of individuals in place from 1991 to 1994 during my college years. Each one of them was a great example of professionalism and helped develop my future career expectations. Last, but not least, I thank my bosses, mentors, and partners during my years at Iberia Tiles. Most of this book's content will be filled with wisdom shared by some of the brightest and most humane people I have known: Rosa Sugrañes, Fernando Vila, Claudio Cuoghi, Don Ramon Sugrañes, Marcelino Sugrañes, and, most recently, Salomon Fadel. I give thanks to all my co-workers, suppliers, and service providers that have shared over twenty years of experiences that will be manifested in this book. It is impossible to name each and everyone, and I expect those unnamed will know in their hearts the lessons we have exchanged through the years. I pray that this book not only will help empower individuals in their professional lives but will also be a spiritual guide. "God, as Truth, has been for me a treasure beyond price. May He be so to every one of us." Mahatma Gandhi.

Preface
Building Great Teams Starts with YOU!

It is not a coincidence that the first chapter of my book titled "Leading by Listening and Obeying" starts with SELF. Teams are made up of individuals and we cannot ignore the role of self. The emotional intelligence that an individual has in recognizing the strengths and weaknesses of self and how those characteristics can help or take-away from a team is important. SELF Love is a must. In order to love others you have to love yourself first. Some individuals love themselves so much that they do not leave room for others. You also need to LOVE what you do.

Business leaders across the globe are continuously making decisions to help move their STRATEGY forward and enlist team members by way of managers and employees to help achieve their goals. During the first 20 years of my professional life I received great counsel from many European leaders. I was also fortunate to create great connections with Asian leaders from China to Taiwan to Singapore and the Philippines. No matter where the leaders were located there were some constant themes that have been captured below:

> "Great leaders should be able to communicate short-term and long-term goals and seek out team member involvement"

> "Great leaders should be able to be trustworthy and loyal to their team members by demonstrating dedication and care for their future"

> "More importantly, the achievements of employees should be recognized"

Within the first Chapter of my book titled "Leading" you will learn more about a formula for individual success that uses the acronym:

Talent
Outlook
Pro-activity

Talented individuals with positive outlooks and pro-active initiatives will be more successful than those individuals that do not use all three of these factor combinations. When TOP individuals are introduced to a team these factors will contribute to the team's success by creating **TOP TEAMWORK!**

Recently, I have been working with the SLIMPACT team at Faour Glass Technologies and was reminded that TEAMWORK Stands for:

Trust
Emotional Intelligence
Alignment
Mentorship
Wow
Open
Results
Kash

Trust is needed in all relationships, business and personal. People are motivated by Sustenance, Security, Satisfaction, and Sense of belonging. Having trust is part of what makes us feel safe. This feeling allows us to act freely without fear. In the professional world, trust is not always a "given". Many organizations will thrive off the lack of trust generated by the "eat or be eaten" survival of the fittest mentality. Unfortunately, when you are part of a great and efficient team there is no room for the lack of trust.

Emotional Intelligence and self-awareness are becoming more and more common place as we educate each other on the sense of self and belonging. Part of our complexity and beauty as human beings are the emotions with which we live and work. Being aware of how our emotions impact others is a very important part of building great teams. Great leaders are capable of understanding their own strengths and weaknesses so that they are capable of minimizing the negative impact that these might have on the team.

Alignment of vision, mission, strategy, and tactics are fundamental to all great and efficient teams. This alignment takes work and a lot of communication. People do not know what they do not know, and it is hard for leaders to sometimes explain to others what is fundamental and elemental to us. Successful teams are the ones that have many opportunities for constant alignment and communication.

Mentorship is important within the team framework because we are at our best when we are helping others to succeed. Many of my workshops will start by asking individuals to name the topmost successful teams, actors, or business leaders. It is amazing how hard it is for people to remember more than a couple of years back to who was at the time. On the other hand people always have an answer and immediate recall when they are asked to name 3-4 people who were fundamental mentors or teachers during their childhood. Mentors and teachers leave a long-lasting mark on each other. We should all have a mentorship/teacher mentality when approaching or working with others. The teacher that I have studied the most is Jesus Christ and there is a great book that I highly recommend called "Lead Like Jesus". I guarantee it will change your leadership perspective.

Wowing the people you serve, lead, help by "doing the common things uncommonly well" is also a great attribute of great teamwork. When the entire team has a philosophy of going over and beyond what is expected to create value for others there is an exponential growth force that propels organizations to the results that are needed.

Open hearts and mentality to external feedback and criticism is another key attribute to building great teams. This is one of the hardest attributes to grasp because our human nature is to become habitual and set in our ways. We have to force ourselves to understand that what we know works today will not always work tomorrow and we have to Listen to others and be willing and open to act on their feedback and input.

Results are a must for any great team that is part of any organization. In sports we know that it does not matter how well or how pretty you play, what matters is how many victories you are able to achieve. The business world is the same way. Creating a team that is obsessed and passionate for delivering results is fundamental.

Kash is needed for any great team to be successful. The world does not function on air alone and organizations need cash in order to fulfill their missions. Teams that are able to provide increased market value and increased premiums will thrive. All others will die.

There are many other attributes that can be discussed when we talk about and define what it takes to build great teams. I encourage you to use these but also create and define your own. Not all teams are alike, and each team has to adapt to their current individual players, mission, and vision. Every organization has a strategy that is established in order to reach a set of desired results and objectives. The members that make up each organization have their own personal drives and talents that help compliment these strategies. Occasionally a team might be missing a particular talent that is needed and these are great moments to create opportunities for people to "step-up" from within or allow us to recruit from outside. With the help of organizations like The Predictive Index, we now have objective methods to identify these gaps. Please visit www.qmresources.com if you wish to learn more about building Dream Teams by using human analytics and software.

I sincerely hope that the following pages help and inspire you to not only become a part of a great team but that you will also feel empowered to become a team leader and builder no matter what you position, or title might be! **Building Great Teams starts with You!**

PROFESSIONAL MANAGERS:

I clearly remember the day 20 years ago when one of my business professors defined Professional Manager as the talented people that are hired to manage capital, aka assets. This definition resonated with me as I had not yet started my own investment strategy and I could clearly see myself as a talented individual that was responsible for capital and assets that our stockholders had entrusted to me.

Management goals vary greatly from organization to organization but there are many underlying objectives that almost all managers must cover to remain viable.

1. Satisfy the investor capital return on investment objectives by way of profits and distributions.

2. Achieve sustainable or increased profits by the generation of real value in benefit of the patrons that subscribe to the business goods or services.

3. Create an environment whereby the team members can align their own personal goals with the goals of the organization.

The third objective is the one that I wish to elaborate on a little further by sharing some of my own personal experiences and views that have helped in my professional life.

Creating a business with flourishing profits and flourishing employee benefits are not mutually exclusive although upon occasion they can be in conflict of one another. We must understand that the business leader has a duty to not only serve his/her own interest but the interest of the organization. On some rare occasions, their own personal interest must suffer for the benefit of the organization because they are called by duty to protect the interest of the organization. By the same token, the employee typically has a need and duty to serve his/her own personal interest first. Finding the balance is the key.

Fortunately, in free market economies, Managers and team members are not alone in helping create the necessary balance. The free market has compensation guidelines that help provide an arena of mutual understanding. There are many mobile applications that capture this data on job posting sites. It is within this framework that I would like to explore the concepts of recruiting and hiring.

RECRUITING & HIRING:

1. **Recruit** people that have individualistic talent that can be used to complement the team as a unit.

2. **Recruit** people that are not only highly skilled but also highly passionate.

3. **Selection** of new team members must be efficient. Today's world of technological advancements can help us reach possible candidates never imagined before. Technology can also help us streamline our selection process. Here are some of the basics that seem like common sense but are often missed.

   a. Properly set duties and expectations by using written job descriptions
   b. Utilize email or web-based platforms to ask preliminary questions
   c. Have an efficient interview process including other team members
   d. Recruit people that have natural behavior drivers that fit the desired role. (Using The Predictive Index tools will help)
   e. Ask for referrals as the candidates will be more reliable than from a global pool.
   f. Check references

4. **Hiring** starts with the leader (you) and the team. Leaders need to be mentally, emotionally, and physically prepared to take on a new team member. Often, many leaders are dis-engaged and removed from the "transactional" hiring process. On the other hand, engaged hiring leaders are capable of motivating and inspiring the team to help make sure that the process is successful. Using the Jim Collins bus metaphor of "getting the right people on the bus" shows that every seat on a bus is surrounded by more seats filled with by other team players. The dynamics between these players are an important key to success.

Successful leaders will enlist the entire team to:

a. Define the job behavior drives as well as the cognitive requirements that the person should have in order to successfully carry out their role. Hiring a person with the wrong behavior drives or cognitive ability will only set the individual and team up for failure.

b. Engage the new team member and help the on boarding process. Leaders that are deliberate in crafting the message that the team should transfer to the new employees will have higher chances of increased productivity.

5. **Hire** people that have realistic personal financial expectations that can be met within your organization.

6. **Hire** people that quickly understand the impact they personally have to the results that the company is needing from them.

7. **On-boarding** is often ignored but equally or more important than the previous areas. Habits and culture will be transferred to the new team members within the first few days. A deliberate training system with a larger participation from successful team members will help set the right tone from the start. Having your most senior leadership spend time with the new members sharing their mission and vision is very inspiring and will be used by the team members when they are present to help "evangelize" your culture with new employees in the future.

8. **Finally, love** the people you hire!

LOVE:

Love is a word that is not commonly used for business relationships. The ancient Greeks would no doubt consider this a tragedy. The ancient Greeks had six different words for love. There are three that I find very apropos to the business world:

Agape: Love that extends to all people and is the root of our charitable nature.

Pragma: Longstanding love leading to compromises rotted in patience and tolerance.

Philautia: Self-love in the healthy sense which yields confidence and ability to give love to others.

Common love is what helps the employer and employee align their personal and corporate objectives. I often compare work relationships to marriages for the many different similarities that can be found from the dating stages unto the commitment stages all the way to the completion stages. Employers and employees court each other initially to make sure that there are enough common interest and objectives to justify a harmonious union. Employees should engage with employers that theoretically meet the requisites that we have in mind. Settling for employers that do not meet the requisites can happen out of necessity but will usually lead to poor performance and engagement. By the same token, employers should be deliberate in vetting their candidates beyond the superficial interview and CV review. When time permits, multiple interviews by multiple people are always recommended. Explore the "deal breakers" during these encounters and hire with a long-term career vision vs. filling a Job void.

Marriages are rarely easy or perfect as they typically require self-sacrifice and constant communication which require effort. Work relationships between team leaders and members often require the same amount of effort. It is up to the leaders to set and communicate the proper expectations with the team members. Team members should conscientiously accept or reject the expectations and be happy with the decision by taking on a zero-complaint mentality. Attitude is everything.

Team and leader relationships can become stale or stagnant as the years go by and complacency sets in. This is the same in our personal relationships. It is up to the business leader to become deliberate in finding ways to ensure that this natural tendency does not set in. People's needs change the same way business needs change and it is important that both grow together in unison. A bit of formality in the leader and team periodic "one-on-one" reviews help keep the communication flowing. Strategic "check-points" or reviews twice per year also help keep everyone on track. The objective is to minimize any surprises that can occur with changes in needs or perspectives from one party to another.

In the end, leaders and teams alike want to be loved. Therapist and life coach, Michael J. Formica, associates this drive to be accepted as part of a core wired instinct attributed to the need for survival. Ultimately it is the responsibility of employers and employees to ensure that they love what they do and do what they love with people they love.

GREAT PEOPLE CREATE GREAT RESULTS:

As business leaders, we are looking to find the Messis and Marinos of the business world so that they can help us win consistently. What do we do when we don't have them, we can't find them, we can't afford them? Being able to succeed despite the circumstances, to me, is the KEY to true leadership... How do we win without Messi? How do we create a winning team without Marino? How do we create a winning team without a Superstar? It is possible and it is done every day!

Great leaders build great teams! Superstars definitely help and we constantly need to be seeking and developing our own. Here are some tips on how to win no matter what:

1. Having the right player in the right position is Key. Messi would not be Messi if he were playing defense. WE all have natural drives that enhance our performance in positions that need our drives regularly. We can all learn to perform in areas that do not come natural. Unfortunately we cannot do this consistently and without expending a great deal of energy.

2. Having a great team of 11 strong and solid players often will be better than having 1 Messi amongst 10 mediocre players. Superstars can sometimes absorb a lot of energy and become hard to manage. Mediocre players will occupy space and prevent you from developing superstars.

3. Have people that want to be like Messi. In other words, have people that strive for excellence and are humble enough to constantly work on enhancing their weaknesses and capitalizing on their strengths.

4. Give people the opportunity to shine. Many times we are so focused on what we are missing that we forget to capitalize on the many assets that we have. Great leaders are "master team builders" and magically bring out the best in everyone.

As a LEADER, I always valued most the team members that were capable of making the best with the resources they had. (Ultimately very few of us ever have the resources we want and the team we want) My best team members were not complacent. They did not complain about their circumstances. They continued striving and searching for excellence, but they were able to do so by looking within and making the best out of the resources they had at their disposition. I hope these words help you continue to strive for excellence and make the best of what you have at hand. One of the tools at your disposition is creating an environment of trust where ideas flow freely and objectives can be shared and delegated amongst team members.

TRUST & DELEGATION:

Leadership delegation and problem solving is not a new topic. There are endless amounts of books and articles that address this topic. My opinion is that today it is more relevant than ever for leaders to become diligent in the way that they delegate, and problem solve. The reason for this is that our demographics are constantly changing, and the new generations of workers will have different needs from their predecessors. As usual, I do not claim to be an authority on any of the subjects that I write... I simply share my experiences. Part of my nature is to avoid truths that are considered to be absolutes. Life has taught me that in most situations, there are many "ways to skin a cat". The views that I share are based on my personal experiences that have provided effective outcomes and will no doubt also be applicable to many situations that you also may be facing.

One of the suggestions that I read recently from a very popular figure suggested that if a leader is not willing to sit down and help "problem-solve" they are indeed part of the problem. In other words, leaders are doing their teams a great injustice when they are not available to help their team members solve problems. This statement could be occasionally true. My experience tells me that it is usually not the case. My experience has shown that great leaders are capable of hiring great people and helping them learn to solve their own problems with minimum help. This is the way that organizations and individuals are capable of growing.

It is true that our new generations are more prone to work as a team and look for constant support. I see this with my 3 adolescent kids.

The i-generation is constantly online in group forums receiving group support or group criticism. They have become more independent in their thinking as they seek to stand out but less independent in their actions as they strive to fit in. They require more help and validation in their day to day living and decision making.

Generalizations are very dangerous. Leaders must understand that "one size does not fit all" and it is important to evaluate and motivate each individual independently for who they are. All individuals are capable of positive contributions. Some individuals contribute more than others. Some environments and leaders are more prone to inspiring effective contributions from team members than others. Here are some tips that helped me create environments of continuous growth and contribution for the myriad of individuals that I have led:

1. Have an "open-door" policy. This does not mean that the door is open all the time. This is more of an attitude than a rule. Thriving team members usually have leaders that are visible and available when needed. It is the leader's job to define the rules of when and how they are accessible.

2. Encourage independent problem-solving. Great leaders are capable of surrounding themselves with great individuals whom many times have better solutions. Make sure your environment is conducive to allowing these solutions to flourish. This includes creating a vetting system so that the solutions are validated. It also means that the environment is sympathetic to mistakes. This means that mistakes are used as learning opportunities vs. judging opportunities.

3. Be diligent in defining the expectations. I personally was brought up in a professional environment where my leader clearly defined the following:

    a. Problems that I was expected to solve on my own.

    b. Problems that I could occasionally solve with support from my team or my leader.

    c. Problems that I never was expected to solve on my own.

Depending on your level of leadership, size of company, and objectives all of the above will vary in degree and magnitude but all are applicable to all organizations at some level no matter what "style" workforce you have.

I would be remiss in stating that leadership styles have a lot to do with innate drives that lead to needs and behaviors that we manifest in our workplace. These drives will make delegation easier for some and harder for others. The motivators will make team collaboration easier for some and harder for others. Managing without knowing your own personal motivators or those of your team members is very difficult and unnecessary. By the same token, complex problem-solving ability is directly correlated to cognitive ability. There are easy and objective ways to understand the uniqueness of each individual's capacity. I am glad to help you learn more about the methods that can help. My web site www.qmresources.com will help guide you to these solutions.

Another important factor that contributes to a team's ability to generate trust is a topic that The Predictive Index CEO Mike Zani brings up in his book "The Science of Dream Teams". In his book Zani with the help of Stephen Baker capture the essence of Team Optimization but also clearly help leaders think about vulnerability in facing their "front shirt" vs. "back shirt" concept.

In essence leaders usually have an impression of who they are which are considered the "front shirt" traits. Many times leaders also have "back shirt" traits that employees assign to the leaders through the grapevine and usually in not such a positive way. Zani and Baker point out the importance for leaders to not only embrace their "front shirt" talents but to also work on the "back shirt" traits that are a drag on the organization by either correcting these traits or refraining from this behavior altogether and having someone else effectively handle the situations where these negative traits commonly surface.

One of the most beautiful things about addressing team strengths and weaknesses is the diversity that can be achieved by having many different styles and tones reach common harmony.

EMBRACE DIVERSITY:

It is no coincidence that a blonde hair, blue eyed, southern American boy that moved to a small town in Spain at the age of six would need to learn to embrace diversity. In 1979 the small town of Xativa had no resemblance whatsoever to the town of Mobile Alabama which I knew up until that time. In the small town of Spain, there were no native boys or girls that looked like me, dressed like me, or spoke like me. I had to acclimate. I had to become one of them. I was very blessed because I have applied these same acclimatation skills to every single person/culture that I have encountered since then. People who know me well know that I love diversity. I love all cultures, languages, and colors without prejudice. I am blessed that embracing diversity is my first nature.

I am a fervid believer that there is always a need for advocacy representing groups that are marginalized or not able to advocate for themselves. I do believe that one of the most daunting challenges of the next 2 decades will be to ensure that the wealth gap does not grow so fast and large that the less fortunate do not have the opportunity to catch up. Those of us who are on the wave of growth need to reach out and pull as many as we can along with us. This is no longer a challenge for nations and governments to fulfill. It is a challenge that businesses across the globe should embrace and meet. In saying this, I will also say for the benefit of my three daughters and in particular for the youngest one… there "is no free lunch" and the world that Karl Marx addressed in 1848 no longer exists. It may seem that some of the same issues exist, but they are much different in nature and therefore the solutions must also be much different.

Charity is healthy, entitlements are not. All good things require work and sacrifice. Occasionally you are given or may inherit good things without much work or sacrifice, but make no mistake, it will take work and sacrifice to keep and grow what you have been given. Work and productivity is the solution, not the enemy.

My objective in addressing this topic is to elevate notions that could be differentiating so that we can seek commonality. This is especially important as I am seeing the co-existence of 5 different generations working within the same organizations. Generalizations are always dangerous and do not always prove to be true. As we look at the nuances of our generation groups it is important to understand that there are always exceptions to the rules, but the most recent generations have a much greater sense of entitlement than the previous generations did. My suggestion is that we replace any sense of entitlements that we may have for an #attitudeofambitiousgratitude.

For the purpose of this article, I will identify the different generations as does www.npr.org in an article called *"From GI's to Gen Z: How Generations Get Nicknames"*:

GI Generation: Born 1901-1924 - They lived through the Great Depression and served in World War II. They grew up in a much different world than what we know today and saw a great amount of physical and economic strife. They are the Great Grand Parents, Grand Parents, and Parents of today's current work-force. Their experiences are real and have an impact on attitudes and perspectives.

Silent Generation: Born 1925-1942 - They are the younger brothers and sisters or sons and daughters of the GI Generation that just missed living the cultural "love" revolution of the 70's. They grew up on modest, hard-working families that believed in following the rules and found opportunities in the post-war world. They are comfortable with structure and following rules.

Baby Boomers: Born 1944-1964 - This generation was born during a time of economic prosperity. They saw the world change with regards to civil rights and actively participated in protesting the US Government intervention in Vietnam. They in my opinion, have set the tone and culture in many of the traditional organizations that thrive today.

Generation X: Born 1965-1979 - This is my generation. We lived through the cultural revolution of the 80's with MTV and the end of the cold war. We were old enough to understand the ethics of the Silent Generation and young enough to adapt to the age of technology driven by the internet explosion. We also lived the impacts of the Great Recession.

Millennials: Born 1980-2000- Much is yet to be discovered with this generation. It has been written that they have a greater sense of entitlement than previous generations. They indeed grew up with full internet access and information on demand. They have a natural sense for technology related advancements and have helped lead much of the current i-revolution.

Generation Z: Born 2001-2013- These are my kids. They are the i-generation. They rely on the internet. They are individualistic. They are technology dependent and benefit from some of the wealth generated by previous generations. They also have an elevated sense of entitlement and have seen insta-success stories created by the virtual viral world. They are starting to enter the workforce.

I mentioned previously that having a sense of "entitlement" is usually NOT healthy. There are certain basic things that civilized human beings expect to have access to: food, water, shelter, safety. Within the United States and most other civilized nations, we also have something similar to the Bill of Rights that expand our expectations to certain liberties and expectations that are general in nature. Although many of these rights may be taken for granted, it is important to remember that they were acquired by great struggle and sacrifice by the generations that came before us. We are the beneficiaries of these efforts and need to work to keep them viable.

Within professional organizational environments entitlements become challenging. Resources are not unlimited and the more pressures we put on organizations to re-distribute their wealth without offering something in return is unsustainable. This is one of the reasons that many of our traditional US businesses in certain industries have closed. It is also one of the reasons that our government has incurred an enormous amount of debt.

Human beings are generally not very easily satisfied. We have a high ability to spend and consume more than what we really need. For this reason, I am encouraging our youth that we become deliberate in fighting this non-satiated appetite and replace it for an "Attitude of Ambitious Gratitude"

When our expectations are low, we are capable of being more gracious for the accomplishments that benefit us. Gratitude is a key component of success and happiness. For those of you that love History as I do., (both history and the History Channel) you can appreciate that during the early existence of humanity there was very little that was granted to newborns. Shelters were rudimentary modifications of sticks and stones provided by nature. Food was hunted or grown, and both required hard work and effort. Safety was self-supplied or provided by those in your family nucleus or clan. In many societies a variety of these notions or all combined are still a reality for many. Working for what we need is part of human nature. Receiving what we need from others is not sustainable because their efforts will not be sufficient to carry the burden of many or they will simply grow tired of working so hard for the benefit of others not willing to contribute.

Within the business world and #attitudeofgratitude toward clients, colleagues, stockholders, and collaborators is one of the ways that I have found can differentiate your organization from others. It can become a competitive edge when it is genuine. It is this attitude to which I contribute the possibility of confronting challenges with a positive outlook and achieving positive solutions. Healthy ambition is also needed. Healthy ambition is what keeps us striving for excellence and looking for new horizons. Ambition is what allows us to become pro-active with our skills and experience.

If we are not ambitious, we do not have the capacity of maximizing our talents and attitude of gratitude. Ambition is like a sailboat engine. Ambition allows us to get to where we want to go faster and without the risk of having currents take us adrift. Ambition is not only about what we want or how bad we want it. Ambition is about how hard we are willing to work to get something that we want. Healthy ambition is good for society.

EMBRACE THE STRUGGLE:

COVID has no doubt created constant and continuous adverse situations that are taking place around the globe. These situations no matter if caused by mother nature or human nature inevitably have an impact on our outlook and demeanor. I personally believe that there are three natural responses that we as human beings have in the face of adversity. I do not believe that there is a particular order for any of the responses and feel that each situation is defined by the personal circumstances and perspectives of each individual. Regardless of the personal responses we might have, there is a professional response that we should have in our organizational environments. I believe that **Lee Iacocca** articulates the response we should have very well:

"In times of great stress or adversity, it's always best to keep busy, to plow your anger and your energy into something positive".

Anger is one of the natural responses that humans have when they perceive that something adverse and unjust is happening. This anger many times can lead to aggression which in turn leads to more adversity.

On the contrary many will react to adversity with sympathy and empathy. Often these reactions lead to positive action by the way of assistance to the people affected by adversity. The outcomes of this reaction are usually positive. Sometimes empathy without action can lead to a negative sense of overwhelming helplessness if not channeled properly.

The third response that I have observed people take is one of apathy. They just don't care. Some people are capable of focusing only on situations that impact them personally and disregarding the adversity being faced by others.

I believe that all three of the responses mentioned above are born within our natural instinct of survival. The truth of the matter is that adversity has been a part of our world since the beginning. Those of us with a sense of the divine understand the merit in the Chinese Yin and Yang theory from the third century BC. This theory explains that interdependency that two opposite forces may have. Fortunately, a majority of humankind over the ages have focused on seeking out a harmonious and peaceful existence. Most have advocated for good vs. bad. The tendency toward peaceful civilizations and democracy has helped this become a reality with minor exceptions. The exceptions have been very painful but have usually allowed us to learn what we do not want for our future.

The majority of the business world functions best in periods of peace and harmony. There are obviously some exceptions to this rule as there are in many things in life but for the most part our "professional" lives are "safe" havens where we can find stability and consistency. The reason for this is that businesses cannot typically survive financially if they are engulfed by much strife and conflict. Businesses are efficient in this manner. The points that Lee Iacocca make are as follows:

Keep Busy: Action and activity help us in so many ways. When we are busy with something productive, we have an easier time forgetting about the negative things that are affecting us. Recently I was impacted by Hurricane Irma while in South Florida during which time I lost power and water for four days. The four days of not having power and running water were minimal compared to the 12 days that I experienced during Hurricane Katrina in 2005. During both of these experiences I spent most of my days physically cleaning debris and most of my nights reading. These activities kept me distracted and occupied. During Katrina much effort was spent on getting my business back up and running. During that time we had at least 80 employees that were depending on our ability to continue operating. We also had at least five times that number of customers that were also in need of us getting operational as soon as possible. Overcoming the challenges of doing so with limited resources was very satisfying. Many times "the harder the battle, the sweeter the victory" holds true.

Plow your anger and energy into something positive: Undoubtedly Lee Iacocca was familiar and therefore specific when using the word "plow". Modernization and machinery now used takes away from the power that this word has for our future generations. During much of our history plowing by hand or by horse required grit, patience, and perseverance. The term also implies that we are to go deeper than just the surface. "Plowing" our emotions and dedication into something positive when facing adversity can change our reality. It can transform something negative into something positive. I do not doubt that Martin Luther King had this in mind with his leadership during the civil rights movement.

Business leaders should be aware that WE play a fundamental role in helping our team members face adversity. Negative reactions beget paralysis, negativity, and low productivity. Positive reactions lead to action, reconciliation, and fulfillment. Here are some of my own personal tips to build upon what Lee Iacocca so eloquently says:

1. **Set aside your personal negative convictions:** You have the right to express what you believe but the workplace is not the best platform for this.

2. **Acknowledge & embrace the adversity:** Acknowledging and accepting the many diverse reactions that people will have will allow them to find their reconciliation. Being dismissive to people's feelings leads to rebellion and divisiveness.

3. **Increase Positive Communication:** During times of adversity, people need to see positive leadership and presence.

4. **Set the tone and agenda:** Leaders have the duty and obligation to set the tone and agenda for the actions that people should take in response to adversity. Do no leave it open for interpretation. Remember that "common sense" is the least common of senses.

5. **Create action plans to keep people busy:** "An idle mind" is not always the "devil's playground" but sometimes it is.

6. **Celebrate victories**: No matter how small a victory may be, it is important to celebrate the achievements so that the teams know that their efforts are leading to positive outcomes.

7. **Lead by example:** People will follow what you do, not what you say.

I will always remember the words from St. Thomas Episcopal Parish Rector, Father Tobin: "A setback is a setup for a comeback". Life will always be full of setbacks. Having the right attitude and leadership approach is what allows us to convert them into comebacks. Please be well amongst all of the adversity you might face and please continue to share the positive that can be found in every situation.

MAKING PROGRESS

I can summarize this collection of articles by re-emphasizing that Building Great Teams starts with YOU! Your attitude, your style, your approach, your communication, your trust, your example, your intelligence, your emotion, your emotional intelligence, your vision, and again your communication. No matter if you are the one leader of the team or a team member these traits are important for you to acknowledge.

How do we know if we are making progress as leaders? In 2018 while working with one of my favorite clients of all time, Eddy Ruiz, and A+E Lifetime Latin America, I came up with a concept that I called:

Leadership
Equity
Asset
Diagnosis

At the very core of this leadership diagnosis is the premise that most times a team member joins a new organization with great excitement and enthusiasm. If we had to give this excitement and enthusiasm a number on a scale from 1-10 it would probably be an 8 or 9. All of the experiences from the time of the job offer to the time of the on-boarding and beyond could either maintain the employee's excitement and enthusiasm or advance it to a 10 out of 10.

The question becomes, how do we measure this in a quantitative way so that we know that we are improving, and it does not become a subjective measure of feeling which is very unreliable.

My solution to the question was by creating a survey. It was a 10 question survey that had questions designed to "measure" this Equity that we had maintained with our new team members. It was very rudimentary, but it worked!

Now, fortunately, great leaders and scientist at The Predictive Index have come up with an Employment Engagement Survey that is very comprehensive and robust that is designed to allow an organization's leadership truly "undress" in front of a mirror and reflect on the pros and cons of the culture that has been created. The objective in the end is to benchmark against other successful entities and pay attention to the areas that need the most improvement.

In my opinion, the process of allowing team members provide honest and objective feedbacks is one of the purest forms of "Leading by Listening and Obeying".

I sincerely hope that you enjoy the following pages that were penned in 2015 but with concepts that are as timeless as the ones that were captured by Sun Tzu in "The Art of War" in the 5th century BC.

INTRODUCTION

In 1994 I graduated magna cum laude from Auburn University Montgomery with a Liberal Arts Degree in International Studies, with a concentration in Hispanic Studies, and a Minor in Business. Having lived most of my childhood years in Spain, my desire upon graduation was to work either with a U.S. company based in Spain or a Spanish company based in the U.S. I pursued opportunities by sending my resume in English and Spanish to as many companies as possible that I thought might hire me and help me to achieve my objectives. One of the resumes was sent to the Spanish Trade Commission in Miami. The resume was intercepted by the acting director. He in turn passed it along to Fernando Vila, CEO of Iberia Tiles. Within the resume I had included my 1992 experience as a Summer Missionary to the World Expo in Seville, Spain. The Director of the Spanish Trade Commission had forwarded the resume to Fernando Vila with a note stating that anyone "selling" religion is Spain must be a good salesman. Without a doubt, God's hand was evident as I was offered a Management Trainee position with Iberia Tiles in October 1994. Little did I know that joining Iberia Tiles would shape my life and my entire career in a very positive manner. My purpose in writing this book is, in part, to help young professionals enhance their future experiences with the tools that God has given them. I will share knowledge that I have acquired over the years. This knowledge will hopefully help catapult their minds to be open to similar experiences they can have. It is much easier to survive the jungle if you can follow the path successfully forged by trailblazers. The idea is to create a workbook manual that not only will cover macro business and life principals, but also will help define day to day habits that will increase chances of success. I sincerely hope that the objective is met and that every single reader will gain as much from it as possible.

BACKGROUND

Iberia Tiles was incorporated in the U.S. in 1979 by Rosa Sugrañes and her father Don Ramon Sugrañes. Don Ramon was a Catalán industrialist from Spain whom I came to consider as an "enlightened" person with experiences and wisdom beyond his time. As a third generation manufacturer of clay products he was not only a visionary within his field, but, more importantly, he had a very deep understanding of human nature. His experience would help shape not only Iberia Tiles, but also Ceramica Sugrañes, Catalonia Distribution, and not the least of these, me. All of the companies mentioned are to this day leaders in their industry.

The title I have chosen for the book is inspired by a Spanish saying that Don Ramón repeated frequently: "Para mandar, hay que obedecer," which interpreted means, "In order to lead, one must obey." Analyzing the deeper meaning of this phrase, I have come to realize that this concept has been the heart of universal teachings for thousands of years, especially in both the Hindu and Christian/Judeo religions. The saying is formed around the basic concept of humility. The ability of shedding the self and seeking the wisdom of others around us is not easy. I believe it goes against the natural human instinct of selfishness. Acquiring the virtue of humility exemplified by many other enlightened individuals throughout history, including Jesus Christ, Mahatma Gandhi, and, more recently, Nelson Mandela, requires mental peace, concentration, and diligence.

A book which I highly recommend as part of any professional's development, entitled Power vs. Force by David R. Hawkins, deals with this concept by explaining the parallels between individual awareness and human behavior. The more aware we become of our conscious states as human beings, the more we are able to control our human behavior and dispel the negative forces that impact us daily. These forces include, but are not limited to, jealousy, fear, hate, greed, and prejudice. The more aware we are of these negative feelings, the easier it is for us to avoid their impact upon us. A higher sense of spirituality is needed in order to fully dominate these feelings. There are many paths that human beings have followed to reach this higher sense of spirituality. Some seek it through meditation. I personally constantly seek spirituality through the power of prayer and the teachings of Jesus Christ. As an active Christian, I am compelled to advocate the path that has worked for me. At the same time, I believe that our God is omnipotent, and, so, I cannot discard the notion that He is able to provide the grace of the Holy Spirit via many different avenues. For the purposes of this book, it is important for the reader to understand that a higher sense of spirituality is achievable. This higher sense of spirituality is what will allow us to truly reach the level of humility needed in order to LEAD by LISTENING and OBEYING.

PART I:
LEADING BY LISTENING AND OBEYING

LEADING

Meriam-Webster has 10 different definitions describing the transitive and intransive verb LEAD. The ones that most describe the meaning used in this book are: (1): to direct the operations, activity, or performance of (2): to have charge of (3): to go at the head of (4): to be first in or among (5): to guide someone or something along a way. There are many different ways and examples that we encounter opportunities to exercise leadership in our life. Some of these opportunities are requested of us by others and some are sought out by us. Whether it be at the age of five as the leader of the line walking from the kindergarten classroom to the lunchroom, or at the age of fifty as an elected public politician, various forms of Leadership are inherit in our society, and are usually valued by society in the form of bestowing respect and monetary compensation on the designated leader. Businesses are very familiar with leaders and there are a countless number of books and examples that relate practices that are successful. This book not only will deal with LEADERSHIP in business, but also in life. I personally think that WE ARE ALL LEADERS of something, whether we are aware of it or not.

My personal experience with Leadership did not really materialize until I started my professional career with Iberia Tiles. During my childhood I was never the constant captain of the soccer team, nor did I have the interest to be a part of the organized clubs during my high school and college years. In retrospect I would consider myself a "connector" and "bridge-maker." I was always interested and involved in building relationships with the people who surrounded me. This trait would later have impact on my future experiences. If you have not yet exercised a leadership role, do not discard the concept that one day you might!

From a very young age I was an avid reader. I highly recommend that everyone try to read at least four books per year, regardless of whether you have a personal affinity towards it or you simply force yourself to do so. Reading has helped me learn about human nature and cultural differences. I have become interested in history and sociology, discovering the ways that human beings will generally act in similar ways to our predecessors. Through historical readings I have been exposed to some of the world's greatest and worst leaders. Whether studying the teachings of King Solomon in the Bible, or the experiences in the lives of Roman Emperors or European Monarchs, or the lives of our American Forefathers, there is always something that we can learn from the trials and tribulations others have faced. From a business perspective I have already mentioned one of the books that I recommend, <u>Power vs. Force</u>. I also recommend <u>The 7 Habits of Highly Effective People</u> by Stephen R. Covey, as well as <u>The Power of Full Engagement</u> by Jim Loehr and Tony Schwartz. You will find in books such as these a consistent theme regarding personal and spiritual edification that LEADS to greater LEADERS.

Although I do not think I personally acted as a leader in the true sense of the word until the beginning of my professional career, I do recognize that from an early age I have been in association with very influential LEADERS that have helped me form a model that I would later try to emulate when my opportunity came. Some of these leaders are mentioned in the acknowledgements. Many others I have observed both near and from afar. It is important for you to continuously identify and observe others from whom you can learn. The wisdom and knowledge experienced is invaluable. I hope to share practical leadership and management concepts that I have learned along the way which I believe you will be able to apply to your own personal situation.

LISTENING

How many times have you been told, "Look at me when I am talking to you." Or, has anyone ever suggested that you were merely "hearing" them speak but not really listening to their words? Being a good listener is in my opinion fundamental to a balanced life. It not only is a necessary attribute in the Business world, but also it enhances our personal relationships. Very often we are so intent on being heard or of sharing our side of the story that we do not generally listen very well. Most of the times we need to "shut up and listen". This concept will be discussed further in the sales section. I will use interactively "listening" and "learning" as synonyms as they relate in this book. Being able to communicate is also a very important trait for leadership. Some of the best historical leaders have been great communicators.

OBEYING

The concept of obeying is one that we are taught from the time of our early childhood development. It is fundamental within our civilized society, intended so that we can all co-exist in harmony. It is fundamental to our humanity and separates us from the rest of the animal world. We cannot do whatever we feel like doing whenever we feel like doing it. Some of us have a harder time with this concept than others. I am sure all can cite examples from our lives when we have rebelled against rules. Very often we rebel or break rules that go against our personal desire of temporary satisfaction or personal advancement. This could also be characterized as selfishness. This book will expose how important it is to OBEY others. Hopefully, I will help show that OBEYING is one of the keys to personal happiness and success. Obeying in the workplace is equivalent to ACTION. We must listen to what is requested of us and act upon the request. As a leader we are to listen to those who surround us and act according to their counsel. As employees or team members we must listen to our leaders and act upon their strategic vision and direction. In life we must obey God and our family members (especially our wives/husbands, or significant others) in order to achieve harmony.

CHAPTER ONE:

LEADING

We are all leaders in certain aspects of our lives. The expectations of leaders vary from situation to situation. There are many books written on the concept of leadership. Following are some of the most important concepts of leadership that I have gathered over the years.

SELF

In order to become and/or to be a good LEADER over a continuous period of time, one must focus on the self. Focusing on the self is obviously a very slippery slope, especially considering that one of my main concepts put forth in this book is the concept of humility. In order to be/become humble, one must relinquish the self and be outwardly focused on others by being empathetic.

The first and perhaps most obvious part of the self to focus on must be the mind. One of the distinctions that separate humans from the animal world is the brain. Our capacity as humans to retain knowledge and grasp deeper intellectual concepts is unique. We must make a point to "feed" our mind with knowledge that can help us succeed in life. The governments in most civilized countries have recognized the value of knowledge and enforce mandatory education for most of one's elementary years. There are some exceptions to this rule, as in some countries the education of women is devalued.

The most developed societies deeply value secondary and higher education, which is manifested in the tuitions being paid at some of the most prestigious institutions. I truly believe that education alone does not necessarily ensure success. I have seen very intelligent Harvard graduates that struggle with the basic concepts of practical life for a lack of common sense while at the same time I have seen very successful 8th grade-educated individuals with a keen common sense, as well as understanding of the human being. The takeaway-point for the reader should be that no matter the level of education, it is important to make sure that we continuously exercise our mind. Much like our physical body needs exercise to stay healthy, our mind also needs activity to stay healthy and continue development. Reading is one way to help achieve this goal. Taking classes from others is also highly recommended as there are advantages achieved through learning from others. Keeping up with technology is a great example of this need. Technology grows and develops so quickly that it can become overwhelming for some of us to keep up with. My kids started using their first computers at the age of three. Currently they use the internet, hand-held smart phones, and tablets for daily learning. This is a huge contrast to my parents' generation which did not own their first computer until their adult years. I am convinced that our generation will be faced with similar advancements of technology, and my grandchildren will be exposed to such and develop a lot quicker than my generation. It is conceivable that at the age of sixty I will be competing in the workplace with a twenty-year-old. This will require that I continue feeding my mind with the things that the next generation is also learning. Otherwise, I will become antiquated and obsolete in my knowledge and skills. Not knowing a skill is NOT an excuse for failure. We must keep up with the skills required of us by society. On more than one occasion I have encountered professionals in the work-force who have not been willing to dedicate the time necessary to keep up with the knowledge and technology required of their profession. They became lazy. Most of them were successful earlier in their careers. They believed that their early success could "carry" them over-- or compensate for their lack of knowledge or development in the new areas. This was and is NOT the outcome. Lack of knowledge will eventually catch up with you. Do not let this happen!

Once the mind is being fed, one can now focus on the body. One of the most influential books that I have read is the previously mentioned <u>Power of Full Engagement</u>. This book relates how important it is for us to focus on physical conditioning in order to be ready for life's demands, whether personal or professional. The authors specifically cite professional athletes as examples of those who focus on the physical well-being of the body, knowing that in doing so, their results will be impacted positively. By the same token, an argument is made that a professional in the business world should also focus on physical well-being. It is logical thinking to assume that physical ailments will impact our physical demeanor as well as energy levels. These physical states will in turn directly impact our ability to lead. For this reason I highly recommend a well-balanced diet as well as a regular exercise routine.

These two components alone will go a long way to help the physical self. Regularly seeing a doctor and taking the necessary medicines or vitamins are also crucial. It is very difficult to be a good consistent leader if one's body is feeble or not functioning at its optimum potential. I have personally been blessed to love sports and physical activity. From an early age I started playing soccer, tennis, and basketball on the streets in Spain. I have continued the love of sports and physical activities throughout my adulthood. Unfortunately there have been some moments in my life when I have been less active than others. It is normal to become lazy and distracted by other activities. The key is our determination to get back on track and to dedicate the time necessary to keep the body healthy. For those who have a hard time doing this on your own, I highly recommend finding a partner or trainer who can help motivate and keep you on track. Team sports are also a great and fun way to stay in shape!

COMMON ATTRIBUTES

Now that the mind and body are being cared for and on track long-term, I would like to focus on some common psychological and philosophical attributes that I have seen manifested in great leaders.

SELF ESTEEM is a very important attribute for leaders. The confidence that we have in our own abilities will define the way in which we act. The people that surround us will perceive the confidence we portray. This in turn instills confidence in others so that they can trust to follow. As the word implies, self-esteem is founded in the self. We need to understand ourselves enough to know our strengths and our weaknesses. Understanding ourselves will allow us to enhance our strengths and complement our weaknesses. We have to understand that each and every one of us has a great deal of value, worth. The people that surround us from early childhood can either enhance or destroy our self-perception. The experiences we live will also affect or define our self-esteem. No matter what your situation or the place where you find yourself, YOU and ONLY you have power over yourself. YOU have the power to shut out or minimize negative feedback while empowering the positive. A very important part of the self-esteem portion lies in our sense of spirituality. Part of the human struggle throughout history has been trying to define one's place within this universe. Our perspective of this will help minimize or maximize our concept of self in our world. From a scientific point of view we are a very small part of the universe. Organized religion or the notion of a supreme being will help us deal with this very important component of our self-esteem. The belief in God who has a plan for each and every one is very powerful in boosting the self. Having a sense of spirituality helps define one's meaning in life and answers the questions that the great existential philosophers have been trying to answer for centuries. Additionally, our sense of spirituality can help boost our self-esteem through prayer and meditation. Those of us with experience in the power of prayer and meditation can attest to the power and tranquility this gives us in our daily lives. With our mind we are capable of understanding the separation of body and soul. We are capable of knowing that our soul drives our being. Our BEING drives our purpose and helps drive our vision and values. Our body becomes the vehicle which God has given us to achieve our purpose. Realizing this helps us KNOW with certainty that WE ARE OF GREAT VALUE. Great companies recognize the fact that human beings are of great value. Our family and friends constantly remind us of the value we provide no matter how they say or show it.

Tip 1. Believe in yourself! Know that you are valuable.

Tip 2. Prayer and meditation can help boost self-esteem.

Having a positive **ATTITUDE** is another attribute common in what I consider a great leader. Although it is true that we can find examples of successful heads of organizations that are not very positive, it is my opinion that these individuals cannot truly be great in all aspects of their lives due to their negativity. Being great and being successful do not always go hand-in-hand. Much depends on the perspective from which we define greatness and success. I would encourage you to think of success as being autonomous in making your own decisions in life and dedicating time to the things that mostly provide you with joy. Success is being able to excel in whatever you decide to dedicate your time to and is greatly defined by your positive impact on the world.

Having a positive attitude is a decision that most of us are able to make daily. With the exception of illness and grief over death, there are very few external factors that should prevent you from having a positive outlook on life. The "life is good" or "la vita e bella" creeds are the ones we should embrace. I always encourage the people I have coached to think of having won or inherited a million dollars. There are very few things that could negatively impact your demeanor in the particular moment of finding out. We can go through life acting as if we just won a million dollars. You will find that going through life with a positive attitude is very powerful. Don't let external factors, such as, things people say, the weather, or set-backs of some kind influence your demeanor. If you are able to view "set-backs as set-ups for come-backs" you will have much more fulfillment in life. Avoid ALL negative influences in your life and surround yourself with people and factors that exude positivity.

Tip 3. Be positive!

Tip 4. Be a million-dollar winner!

Tip 5. Avoid negativity!

Living a **BALANCED** life is another attribute found in leaders. The book, The Power of Full Engagement, by Jim Loehr and Tony Schwartz, is very good in describing the impact of balancing body, mind, and spirit. The body is our vehicle to life. We must take care of our body in order to live life to the fullest. Professional athletes are very committed to exercise routines. They also follow carefully planned diets. Those of us in the work force must do the same if we want to excel in our profession. It amazes me to know that a large majority of professionals do not realize the importance of preparing their body, mind, and spirit for the needs required by their professions. Most professionals will work anywhere from 40-70 hours per week. How do we prepare for this high intensity, high stress requirement? We should definitely perform regular physical activities. I suggest that you find activities that you enjoy and can perform at least 3 times per week. You might also find friends to perform these activities with so that you might have a support group to help motivate and encourage your progress. It is also very wise to take breaks during the workday so that you can take a walk and clear your head. Some of us are required to work long, continuous hours in small spaces. Getting up and stretching and/or walking will help the body, as well as the mind and spirit. Following a healthy diet is another component to living a balanced life. All of us are impacted by certain foods in different ways. [Finding the foods that fit your particular needs could take some time and may even require the help of a professional nutritionist or doctor, but once you identify them and stick to them, you will find that it is well worth the effort. I particularly work well with high protein/ vegetable and moderate carbohydrate diets. We all should include the necessary food groups and nutrients recommended by our doctors, but I try to minimize all processed foods, sugars, and alcohol. I do not recommend cutting these foods out altogether as it is very difficult to live a balanced life without occasional birthday cakes and ice cream or having a beer while on a fishing trip. The important point is to use these in moderation and stay away from large quantities of high calorie, high fat, and high sugar content foods which are not necessary. If you are more than 20 lbs overweight, consider changing your lifestyle today. Seek out help from a professional if you cannot do it alone. Being overweight is not good for you medically and will definitely reduce your performance in life.

Feeding your mind and spirit is another component of living a balanced life. I am fortunate to come from a family of readers on my mother's side. Reading has been easy for me since my early childhood years. Reading helps keep the mind active. Reading also helps gain knowledge. It also helps us learn about cultures and experiences foreign to our own. This understanding helps us relate to each other and become more tolerant of others. Through history we are able to learn from our past mistakes and work together so that they are not repeated. Reading and learning throughout life are also crucial to making sure our professional skills are kept up to date.

At the age of 23 in 1996 at Iberia Tiles, I was promoted to the Sales Management Team comprised of six individuals ranging from 30-50 years in age. I was able to experience the challenges faced by the older members who had limited exposure to computers and spreadsheets. It was much more challenging for them to keep up with the demands of the generation customer base. They were also challenged in being able to take advantage of the technology that would help them become more efficient. In present day 2014, at the age of 40, I can see that my kids will communicate and relate to each other much differently than did my generation. This will definitely impact the professional world and require that we keep up with the younger trends as eventually those who comprise this younger generation will be working with, for, above, or against us. This will require dedication and effort due to the fact that we are creatures of habit. Most of us are also lazy and will take the path of least resistance. As I said earlier, I highly recommend you read at least four books per year and keep up with current technologies no matter whether you think you will use or need them in the future.

Last but not least, I would like to address my experiences with keeping a healthy spirit. I feel fortunate to have learned how to keep a healthy spirit much younger than average. Recently I was with a friend who defined the early stages of life as being filled with excess and excitement while he described our latter years as being dedicated to substance and meaning. The spirit is our inner being of self-conscience that helps us determine between right and wrong. Our spirit also provides the sense of existence and yearning for explanations in life. I have already written about the importance of self-confidence. Feeding the spirit regularly not only will help our self-esteem, but it also will help us live fuller and happier lives. How do we feed the spirit? Prayer and/or meditation are two ways to feed the spirit. Both of them will help us clear our mind and negative thoughts created by our day to day lives. Negativity is manifested in many different forms but commonly experienced as anger, greed, envy, fear, and selfishness. [This is a repeat of some of your same thoughts on p. 4]. These negative forces are at work daily and can be caused by ourselves and those around us. With the right frame of mind we are able to minimize these forces and replace them with kindness, love, and understanding. You might think that this sounds a little banal, but, I invite you to try my suggestions and I guarantee that you will agree with me.

I suggest you pray and/or meditate at least three times per day. It is best if you dedicate at least 5-10 minutes of un-interrupted quiet time for this discipline. During this time you should breathe deeply and clear your mind of all of the negative things that have been bothering you. I typically try to embrace and imagine the worst negative scenarios in my mind so that I can embrace them and release them on my own terms. This prevents me from reacting in the heat of the moment to experiences that might have otherwise bothered me. For example, during a recent family trip, we had erroneously booked a very tight connection between Dallas and Miami and later from Miami to Spain. In preparation for this we planned not to check our luggage so that we could have our carry-on items s with us at all times (the airline had lost our luggage twice during similar trips). While boarding in Dallas, we were forced to check our carry-on luggage due to a lack of space. My wife was furious. I was not. The reason for this is that prior to the trip I had mentally thought of all of the possible negative scenarios. I embraced them, accepted them, and moved forward by giving thanks to God for His many blessings upon me and my family. I mentally decided to deal with my luggage being lost, my connection being missed, and our trip postponed. For this reason I was able to relinquish control and submit myself to the mercy of God's will for my trip and be happy in doing so. Try something similar and you will see that it works!

When you are capable of relinquishing control continuously for everything in life, you will find that you are capable of managing your emotions. You will understand that no matter how hard you try, you cannot control life. You can and should prepare yourself for all possible outcomes which will prepare you for increased success no matter what life might throw your way!

Tip 6. Perform physical activity often.

Tip 7. Follow a healthy diet.

Tip 8. Feed your mind through reading and learning.

Tip 9. Feed your spirit through prayer and meditation.

Tip 10. Be kind and loving toward others, no matter what!

Tip 11. Imagine the worse outcomes and prepare for the best!

WISDOM and VISION go hand-in-hand for leaders. Many leaders are wise by nature. They are born with the God-given gift of wisdom. This wisdom generally provides great perspective on situations and helps one to understand different types of people. Wisdom provides calm during stressful situations and helps set a tone of comfort for others. Being wise helps define a vision. Visions can be personal or organizational. Visions are generally used to define purpose and create objectives for people to follow and believe in. Leaders have to define vision. Organizations without a vision for an extended period of time will eventually meander and die.

Wisdom can be attained via knowledge and experience. It can also be enhanced by surrounding ourselves with other wise men and women. It has been my experience that every single person has something wise to share. As my great history professor Dr. Ramirez would say, "It is our job to become like sponges and absorb the wisdom and knowledge shared by others vs. being like a duck which repels the water and glides through life".

Tip 12. Be like a sponge, not a duck.

Tip 13. Be wise by attaining knowledge and experience as well as surrounding yourself with other wise men and women.

Tip 14. Create a vision for yourself and your organization.

Great leaders create great **TEAMS**. Leaders are continuously recruiting and networking with individuals who can contribute to the advancement of the organization. I personally keep a list of three individuals who can replace any position crucial to the success of my organization. Great individuals make great organizations with very little effort. It is our job to identify great individuals for the right position. Having a great individual in a wrong position can be crippling to the organization. Finding the right individual for the right position, although very time consuming, will be a great catalyst to success for the organization.

There are four different areas that I focus on when recruiting:

1. Talent
   a. Aptitude
   b. Family background
   c. Education
2. Experience
3. Outlook = Attitude
4. Pro-activity

All four are crucial to the success of an individual, and, thus, a company. The lack of any one of these components will set a team member up for possible failure within an organization. Excellent individuals will encompass all four areas. On occasion we will be forced to create great teams with individuals that meet three of four criteria. I do not suggest anyone be hired with only two of the four prerequisites. In order to manage this process we must define what we expect from each individual and each position. Having clearly defined job descriptions will help us do this. Understanding different characteristics that influence positive performance also will help us identify whether our potential team members possess these traits. There are many tools available to help us measure individuals. I will

13

discuss some of the tools with which I have had experience, with the understanding that there are many other similar tools that may perform the same functions.

In order to team build, leaders need to create a filtering/interviewing process to identify the individuals believed to be possible candidates. This task can be very overwhelming depending on the state of the market and number of applicants. Larger organizations might use

Human Resource departments to help with this process. Smaller organizations might use PEO's, Recruiters, and/or support staff to help this process. The clearly defined position needs to be published in a manner that will reach a targeted audience of potential recruits. Referrals from well-known and trust-worthy individuals, and/or clients, are usually very good ways to Identify new candidates. Other conventional methods of job postings in newspapers and Web-based entities also can be effective when publicizing the need. Every candidate should be required to send a resume which will include contact information and references. The resumes should be reviewed with the objective to identify components of talent, education, and experience that meet the job requirements. During the review of the resume it is important to know that it is natural for most resumes to contain *fluff*. *Fluff* is what I describe to be exaggerations of relative truths. Candidates are trying to enhance their appeal so that organizations will see them as the appropriate pick for openings from a pool of people. I personally do not mind candidates to include fluff in their resumes as long as they are not flagrant lies and do not directly impact the possible performance of the job. Dishonesty is a zero tolerance standard. The acceptability of degrees of *fluff* needs to be established by the leader. I personally accepted very little *fluff* from possible bookkeepers, but would consider *fluff* from sales representatives.

Examples of *fluff* I have encountered are as follows:

<u>EXAMPLE A</u>

CONTROLLER – Building Materials Distribution Corporation – 2005–2008

• Responsible for reducing expense from $1,000,000 to $500,000 per month. (**FLUFF**)

REALITY: *The housing market went through a drastic crash and the building of new homes came to a halt. The organization had to reduce the number of locations from 10 to 5 which resulted in an organic reduction of expenses. The fluff is leading one to believe that the Controller was entirely responsible for reducing expenses by his own ability to increase efficiencies.* (**Possibly acceptable as long as it was clarified during the interview process and the potential Controller explains that the market conditions were an important factor in this statement**)

• Oversight of three senior accountants and three bookkeepers responsible for A/R, A/P, and financial reporting (**FLUFF**)

REALITY: *The individual had the title of Controller but reported to a CFO which also managed the other department individuals. The controller was mainly responsible for financial reporting and bookkeeping.* (**Not Acceptable as it is a blatant lie which enhances his/ her experience and is mis-leading to a point that can impact possible performance as a department Controller.**)

<u>EXAMPLE B</u>

ACCOUNT MANAGER – XYZ LLC. – 2009 to Present

• Oversight of 40 accounts and recognized as top revenue generator over last three consecutive years. (**FLUFF**)

REALITY: *The individual was among one of five top revenue generators and reached his budget three of the last four years.* (**Acceptable as the embellishment of his/her achievements was ambiguous and did not directly contradict the possibility of him/her being a revenue generator**)

The most crucial aspect of identifying fluff in a resume is being able to ask the right questions in order to understand the type of individual that you are dealing with and whether the fluff will work to the benefit or the detriment of the organization. Sales people that I hired using fluff were less credible and monitored more closely with regards to their pricing and discount needs vs. those who were straight shooters from the beginning.

Once the resume has been reviewed and the candidate is among the potential candidate pool, I suggest that the organization send them an online or e-mail questionnaire. Within this questionnaire you will include generic questions applicable to all candidates. You should also include questions that are meant to further clarify performance or possible fluff. I like including an essay component so that you allow candidates to freely elaborate expressively. This will give you insight to their aptitude and expressiveness as well as to their ability to organize thoughts and formulate proposals. Here are examples of some possible generic questions with the explanations for each in bulleted italics:

1. **What do you consider to be your greatest strength?**

   - *This will help you learn of one of the candidates possible strengths. It also will give you some insight as to the capability of the candidate to "sell" themselves. You also will get some insight to their state of mind and egoism.*

2. **What do you consider to be your greatest weakness?**

   - *This not only will help you understand a weakness that might potentially impact performance but it also will give you some insight to the candidate's humility and integrity. Many people will struggle with this answer as it is hard for them to identify a weakness, or they have been coached to not show signs of weakness.*

3. **Describe your dream job in a paragraph. Include the title, size of organization, income potential, amount of direct reports, as well as duties and objectives.**

- *This open-ended essay type question will give you some insight as to the future aspirations of a candidate, as well as expectations. I believe it is crucial for an organization to match candidate expectations with those of the organization. This obviously depends much on the job description and longevity expectations. Temporary workers and part-time seasonal positions are not impacted by longevity.*

4. **If we asked you to give us a copy of your W2's for last and year before last what would they show as gross wages: Last Year $_____ Year Before Last $_____**

- *This will be very valuable information in the event you are interested in making a job offer. It will let you know whether your compensation is competitive or in the realm of what the individual expects. I am always fearful of individuals who have earned a lot more or a lot less than the offer you plan to present.*

5. **Describe yourself in paragraph form:**

- *This will allow the candidate to freely describe themselves which will occasionally yield insight that would not have otherwise been attained in an interview.*

6. **Do you prefer to work alone or within a team?**

- *This will allow you to understand whether the position available is paired with the individual's desires. These desires are commonly unclear. Often individuals will express that they like working alone and on teams. Follow up questions during the interview process will be required to hone in on a definitive answer. Some individuals can successfully perform in both environments.*

7. **Describe your 3-year professional goals:**

- *This will help you identify the candidate's ambition.*

8. **Describe your 5 year personal goals:**

- *This will help you understand the individual's aspirations.*

9. **Do you prefer a Micro-manager who oversees minor details or do you prefer a Macro- manager who helps you define goals and will sporadically check to make sure you are on track.**

- *This will help you understand how to best motivate this individual if he/she becomes part of your team.*

10. **Describe some of your hobbies.**

- *This gives insight to some extra-curricular activities that may or may not impact performance.*

Once these questions are answered and reviewed the surviving candidates should be interviewed by phone to ensure that the opinions generated from the written questions are supported over the phone. This should be a quick 5-10 minute conversation. If the phone interview is positive, you will want to set up a physical face-to-face interview immediately. If negative, you can let the candidate know that you are in the phone interview phase which will take approximately two weeks. Inform them that upon completion they will be called for a follow-up meeting or be let known that the position has been filled. This will allow the door to remain open for possible future candidacy if the individual is not the best for the position at hand, but good enough for future consideration. It also will help you shift some of the discomfort of letting a person know that you have decided they are not right for your position. This can have a negative impact on the individual and the organization if the individual is a possible future marketer of the organization. I highly recommend that you get back to 100% of your candidates. It is very poor etiquette to not be responsive to candidates and can have an impact on future prospecting.

The physical interviews are the last part of the filtering process. I recommend two physical Interviews, if possible. For executive positions both are crucial to success. The first would be a formal interview in an office setting with possibly the leader and/or other colleagues and/or HR

Representatives present. Group interviews can be intimidating but are very powerful as many perspectives are necessary for complete analysis. It also "takes a village" once the candidate is hired, and you will want some of your "villagers" participating in the process. Solo interviews are also acceptable. During the formal interview you will identify all four of the characteristics previously mentioned, or lack thereof, and try to re-enforce any of the gaps or inconsistencies left by the filtering process. I like creating comfortable environments where the candidate can relax and be themselves. Candidates that are in dire need of a job can be very nervous and uptight. Younger and less experienced candidates also can be very nervous. I always recommend finding ways to make the candidate feel comfortable enough to open up about themselves. This is best achieved by creating a comfortable non-threatening environment. One of our objectives during the interview process is to find out what the candidate has not yet told you or is trying to withhold from you. Another is to get to know the candidate's personality, as well as their ability or lack thereof to perform under stress, or their ability to deal with conflict. Be prepared to make job offers on the spot for candidates that are clear fits for your organization. Have a prepared formal offer letter that allows for the candidate to sign the acceptance of the offer. This process will help reduce losing candidates to an active employment market where there are a number of organizations trying to hire from the same pool of candidates.

Understanding your candidate's attitude is one of the primary focuses of the interview process. Measuring attitudes of individuals whom we do not know is very difficult. We should realize this and prepare ourselves to conduct an exhaustive search and filtering process which will require time and patience. It also will require objectivity. Some of the worst hires that I have made in my career have been done with haste and relying on my "gut" feeling. The chances of failure are high even with proper due process. Leaders must invest time with the hiring process as the new team members will greatly impact the organization in the future. If the leader does not invest the time it is very unlikely that anyone else will. Even larger organizations with very structured and organized Human Resource departments can fail in this area. They can get mixed up in the bureaucratic processes while losing sight of the objective needs. Many organizations need Human Resource departments to help with the demands of recruiting and legal requirements. They can be very helpful and efficient in helping hire a prospective team member. It should, although, always be done in tandem with the direct leader of the department for which the new team member will work. During the filtering process there are certain characteristics that individuals with positive attitudes will have. A positive attitude will not ensure success, but, an absence thereof will definitely ensure failure.

The following formula is one I have used for Success in identifying and enlisting **TOP** performers:

Talents +
Outlook +
Pro-activity = **SUCCESS**

Talented individuals with a positive outlook who are pro-active will be successful. Talented individuals with negative outlooks can potentially be successful economically, but will probably lack in happiness that a positive demeanor brings. Talented individuals that have positive outlooks and do nothing with their talent will not be successful as they will not share their talents or outlooks with the rest of the world. All three of the components are important in achieving success long term. It is important to recruit individuals based on this formula.

During the filtering process we are mainly trying to identify whether the individual has the talent and experience required to perform the job. The Judeo-Christian belief system (which I share) teaches us that Talents are given to us by GOD. Others may view these talents as the ones that we are born with. There is no doubt that some of us are born with the ability to sing and others are not. Some of us are talented artists while others are not. Some of us are quicker with numbers while others are great literary intellectuals. By the same token, there are other traits that we are born with that form part of our personality and allow us to perform certain tasks with more ease than others. I will refer to this natural ability as aptitude. I currently marvel at the variety of aptitudes that offspring from the same parents can have. I see manifested in my eldest daughter a great voice and aptitude for art and design. My middle daughter is a great and natural athlete with a buoyant and vibrant personality. My youngest daughter has the memory of an elephant and is devouring books way beyond her years. These aptitudes may or may not help them in their future careers, but should enhance future opportunities and happiness. These are the types of talents that leaders want to identify in their team members. These talents can help the organizations thrive. By the same token individuals are usually most happy doing things for which they have natural aptitudes.

Family background is also a very important indicator of talent. There are certain traits of individuals that are learned from the context of their family environment during early childhood development. These traits and behaviors are usually internalized and potentially replicated later in life. There are always exceptions to these rules, but they are true in a general sense. I personally come from a family of hard-working, dedicated, and ethical individuals. My Dad, brothers, uncles, and cousins all have a similar work ethic which I believe stems from my Granddad and possibly even from my Great- Granddad and beyond. Growing up in a household with positive behavior role models is very powerful. Obviously, there are individuals who are not as fortunate as to have this positive re-enforcement at home during early developmental years. Still, they are capable despite the lack of positive role models and in many cases, the presence of negative behavior role models to overcome these adversities. It is important for leaders to understand the dynamics that individuals bring to organizations.

There are many other examples of learned and/or inherited family aptitude and behaviors that are part of the talents that individuals possess. There are many tools that help organizations measure and identify some of the God-given talents and the talents that are passed on through families. There is one that I have used for twenty years and have lived by its accuracy most of the time, which is called the Predictive Index (PI). It is a measuring tool developed by very smart individuals that is capable of projecting our natural talents. I highly suggest you look into this tool or a similar tool to be used during your filtering process. Essentially the PI establishes via a series of adjectives whether an individual is naturally: outgoing vs. introverted; detail-oriented vs. aloof; calm vs. active; or, team-oriented vs. me-oriented. The objective for leaders is to place individuals in roles that naturally match the individual's profile. Most introverted individuals are capable at some points in their lives to act extroverted out of necessity. The human is resilient and can adapt. Unfortunately, putting an introverted individual in an extroverted sales role will eventually create stress for the individual and the organization, as the individual will constantly have to work hard at being something that he/she is not. It is much better to find a naturally extroverted person for a sales position. By the same token, you rarely will see a naturally extroverted and gregarious salesperson having to continuously book debits and credits as an accounting manager. They are probably capable of doing the job but will not be happy doing so for an extended period of time. The Predictive Index will help organizations identify these natural talents.

Education is also a very important contributor of talents. It is said that "knowledge is power". Humans are capable of learning almost anything despite their God given talents. Having lived over twenty years in Miami, I have evidenced what a highly educated Cuban immigrant population is capable of achieving. Many doctors, lawyers, and educators were forced to abandon their previous careers and learn new trades or careers for their new lives in the U.S. You will find great scientists who have become great accountants or the most knowledgeable philosophers that now own truck companies. This shift was driven by need but is a great example of human resilience and the capacity to learn. Education is important when hiring. All jobs should have pointed educational requirements. It is not necessary to have a college education to be a truck driver. But it sure helps to have a college education when you started driving trucks and now own a nationwide trucking company. There are many examples of individuals that have not pursued higher levels of education and are very successful. It is clear that higher levels of education are not absolutely necessary for success. By the same token, what we learn during our education is very important for most careers as it enhances our global knowledge. There are many daily applications for what we learn. One of the most important aspects of having an education is the fact that you have proven the ability to learn new subjects. You have proven that you have been required by an institution to learn and test under pressure. This will help you later with the pressures that your career can demand. Presenting sales budgets in a timely manner or making a presentation of a new product to a group of individuals is always easier for individuals who during their education have had to meet deadlines or speak in public. Individuals who have achieved high grades during their education could possibly be fast learners. They have also typically experienced some sense of work/reward relationship which can be useful in their career motivation. During the interview process it is very difficult to subjectively measure how much of an impact a candidate's education will have on their future performance. Iberia Tiles used a test called the Wonderlic that helped establish objective benchmarks for us. The test creators established grading standards that were typically acceptable or needed for certain jobs. The test is composed of logical and mathematical questions that need to be answered in 12 minutes. The correct answers would give us a grade that would be used to benchmark against other possible candidates. This would give us a sense of the candidate's education or lack thereof. Most importantly it would let us know if the candidate had the sufficient capacity to perform the functions required by the job for which we were hiring. Occasionally we would hire certain individuals that did not meet the Wonderlic benchmarks only to later find that the individual had a serious limitation. Once it was explained to me that the Wonderlic measures the human "horsepower" -- the capacity to generate brain activity at the level necessary for certain jobs. No matter what test or method you use it is important to make sure your candidate is capable of performing his/her job.

Once we have exhausted identifying the candidate's natural talents and educational background, we can now focus on the Experience portion of the resume. Experience is not required for all positions, but it is very helpful for most. Having experience can be both negative and positive depending on the habits established with other organizations. It is the leader's job to identify whether the candidate's experience is positive or negative. It is also important to discuss actual details of the candidate's experience to get a feel for whether past experiences will be similar to future ones. It is also important to identify how the candidate acted or performed in the functions that were required of him or her at other organizations. This is the area where "fluff" can be impacting. It is important for the leader to not take the experience for face value but to identify whether the candidate is capable of handling the job that is required by the hiring organization.

All along the filtering process the leader should be measuring the candidate's outlook or attitude. This is one of the most important components of a candidate's contribution. In a general sense I have always recommended to hire based on attitude. Background and experience are very important but candidates lacking skill sets can be trained. Obviously, it is always preferred to find individuals with all of the necessary components, but a positive attitude is a must no matter what the position. Outlook and attitude cannot be learned. You either have a positive outlook or you don't, and this is a personal decision that we all make daily. I previously shared the example of imagining having won or inherited a million dollars. There are very few things that could counter the happiness that most people would feel in that situation. The challenge of measuring attitude during the filtering process is that candidates will generally show you a positive outlook. They know that they are being evaluated and will commonly be positive and friendly. What leaders really want to know is if they can be positive and friendly for a consistent amount of time and under stressing circumstances. This aspect is hard to measure objectively. I sincerely believe that one of my God-given talents is having a great understanding of human nature. It has been relatively easy for me to understand a candidate's demeanor and very rarely have I failed identifying candidates with positive attitudes. For leaders who have a harder time reading or understanding this component of individuals, I suggest that you create some role-playing situations or ask candidates pointed questions about uncomfortable situations from their past and ask how they reacted to the situations. You will be surprised what you will find. Recently I participated in an interview for a sales candidate who had great experience and seemed to be a perfect match for the job during the first half of the experience and educational review. He was nice, positive, and seemed to be outgoing and secure in himself. When we dove into his reasons for leaving his current job, we saw a totally different side of his attitude as he described his negative feelings toward his current manager. His lack of respect and prejudice toward his new, female, Latin boss was amazing. He told us exactly what he felt about this obviously stressful situation in a very negative manner. He was clearly not an individual we wanted on our team. Never underestimate the power of a positive outlook no matter how good the candidate is in the other areas.

Individuals that have great talent, experience, and outlook will not achieve anything if they do not share these attributes with others. In order to become successful one must act. One must put his/her talents to use. In most cases acting alone is not sufficient. In most cases the individual must be pro-active. The difference in being re-active or pro-active should be quite obvious to most. Unfortunately it is our human nature to be "lazy" and seek the paths of least resistance which for some individuals means doing just enough to get by. I would say that the majority of our workforce is made up of these type individuals. It is not that they are bad individuals. They just don't have the motivation to do any more than what they are doing. It is the leader's job to identify these individuals and look for the ones that are naturally motivated to help move the organization forward. Some positions require a higher degree of self-motivation and pro-activeness than others, but generally speaking it is crucial to find proactive individuals. You will find that the most successful organizations have a higher percentage of these individuals. Reactive individuals can become mediocre which is the most difficult type of an individual for a leader to deal with. They are not bad enough to fire but are not good enough to help move the organization in the right direction. These people should be replaced ASAP otherwise you will find yourself with a mediocre organization that becomes stagnant. In today's active market being stagnant is equivalent to death. The organization will eventually fail because it will not be able to pro-actively keep up with the demands of the marketplace. Eventually a competing organization or many competing organizations will do so and eventually your mediocre organization will fail. Always look for pro-active individuals that are able to use their talents in a positive manner.

Once again, be prepared to offer jobs to candidates that meet your requirements on the spot.This will set a tone for the candidate to show that you are a pro-active organization. It also will prevent you from losing candidates to the competition in active employment markets.

Tip 15. Establish job descriptions and guidelines for positions.

Tip 16. Work in tandem with Human Resources to identif prospective team members.

Tip 17. Establish a good filtering process to identify potential candidates.
   a.   Have all candidates send resumes with references and contact information.
   b.   Identify personal talents.
   c.   Don't take experience at face value and dive into experiences.

Tip 18. Look for individuals with positive attitudes.

Tip 19. Hire individuals that are pro-active.

Recruiting and hiring is only the first component of successful team building. One of the most important contributions that leaders can have is the development (training) of their team members within their necessary roles. It is important for leaders to create an organizational chart that addresses every aspect of the needs of the business. Clearly defined organizations are able to work more efficiently as each and every team member will understand their role and contribution within the organization and avoid duplicity of functions. Once an individual is hired it is important for the leader responsible for the candidate's performance to ensure that the individual is properly trained. The training process cannot be solely the responsibility of the leader, but the leader is required to closely supervise the training process to ensure that the candidate is able to perform within a specific amount of time. To this end, I suggest that the leader write down every single component of the member's training process and continuously review their development until completion.

Example:
+++
Candidate: Name (Carlos Gilbert)

Objective	Trainer	Proficiency	Comments
Learn Products	Mary	(filled by trainer)	(future follow up)
Learn Software	Jerry	(filled by trainer)	(future follow up)

+++
I suggest that the leader schedule to spend the first two days of the candidate's incorporation to the organization with the person. During this time it is crucial to set the pace of expectations and communicate the corporate culture and historical components of the organization which not only will give the candidate a sense of the greater objective but also allow them to feel positive about their decision of joining an organization with a clear sense of purpose. It is important for the organization to communicate its creed and expectations of the candidate. The creed that I developed over the years for my team members is as follows:

"I am an extraordinary individual that is part of an extraordinary organization of people with common goals of excellence. I will not complain. I will not make excuses. I will be responsible for my actions. I will help encourage others to succeed. I will learn to make my own decisions. I will live by my own decisions. I will embrace the encouragement and feedback I receive from my colleagues and mentors. I will recognize failures and celebrate success. If I cannot continuously deliver excellence, I will help my team find a solution to my performance deficiencies. I will accept constructive criticism gracefully and will communicate criticism of others kindly. I expect respect and will be respectful of others. I accept humility. I accept the challenge of learning from others and also teaching others what I know. I will put forth the effort required of me. I will not be envious or condescending of others. I will refuse gossip. I am confident in my ability. I will perform happily and enthusiastically. I will take care of my body, mind, and soul

both personally and professionally. I will work diligently and avoid idleness.

I am an extraordinary individual doing the common things uncommonly well to the benefit of my colleagues, vendors, clients, and organization."

Every organization should develop a creed or manifesto that works for their particular market or circumstances. Within the creed that I developed it was important for me to make clear that we consider our team members as being extraordinary individuals that are part of an extraordinary organization. This was a very powerful part of our culture. Knowing that the market is full of mediocre individuals gave us a sense of purpose with the most mundane routines such as answering phones or sending quotes. We strived to do everything with excellence. Eventually the market will perceive this.

Not allowing individuals to complain or make excuses for their actions sets the tone for personal responsibility. Complaints become negative and demoralizing. Taking personal responsibility for our actions is very difficult. It seems that almost from birth we are blaming others for our actions. My daughters do it every day. Blaming others and making excuses should not be allowed in an organization. It is unhealthy. We should take responsibility for our failures and successes. When failing we should recognize it and find solutions.

Helping others to succeed will create a sense of unity and help the organization spread the responsibility for success. Requiring individuals to make their own decisions is not always a requirement for all jobs and organizations but for me it was important to make sure that they eventually develop a certain sense of independence being that most organizations cannot make all decisions for their individuals. There has to be a sense of autonomy. Being able to receive constructive criticism is part of listening. Doing so with a positive attitude is crucial as defensive individuals will typically not be able to take corrective measures necessary to advance in their careers. Manifesting that teamwork is expected allows the individual to reduce the selfishness of having to conquer the world on their own. Working and learning in an environment of respect and kind regard for one another helps create a harmonious environment.

Once the individual creed has been explained and accepted by the candidate it is important to set forward the corporate values of the organization. These values will help establish "rules of engagement" for the team members. It is always best for the individual leader to be able to communicate the values, but eventually the entire organization will be capable of sharing them as they will be part of the organization's DNA.

Here are some examples:

1. We live with integrity.
   - Everything we do has to be done with high ethics.
   - We will not be dishonest with our clients, vendors, or colleagues.

2. We make unbreakable commitments.
   - Keeping commitments carries a premium in the marketplace.
   - The organization will back up the commitments of one team member.

3. We work as a team.
   - Individually we are weak, together we are strong.
   - Internal conflict will not be tolerated.

4. We work with design.
   - Everything we do will reflect our sense of design.
   - The way we dress, present products, etc. will be done so with high standards.

These core values will help create uniformity for the team. They will be the compass for decisions to be made in the future. In addition to the core values, it is also important for leaders of organizations to set codes of conduct and dress. Typically, I have incorporated these codes into employee handbooks. The handbook is something that is very easy to develop and does not have to be a long document. It should be given to the candidate the day of hiring and reviewed with them during the first day of their training. I highly recommend that you have the employee sign acceptance of the handbook as well as initialing the important clauses regarding liable conduct such as drug use and harassment. This will help formalize the acceptance of these codes and there will be no doubt whether the employee read the information or not in the event of future situations. I recommend you always prepare for the worst and hope for the best. During my career, I have had very few instances where I had to use these signed documents, but I was surely glad I had them when the occasion arose.

Once the leader has completed his/her two days with the new team member it is now time for the rest of the organization to participate in helping develop the individual. I highly suggest that you plan for the new individual to spend time with every single department that will impact his/her job performance. The time spent up front will accelerate the candidate's performance in the future. It is much easier to gain this knowledge in the beginning when the candidate has not officially started his/her functions. Once they start their duties it is almost impossible to extract them from the day to day obligations in order to positively benefit from the time with other departments. During the time in other departments the new team member not only will learn about practical things needed to perform their job, but they also will learn how to deal with the different personalities that are found within the organization. A healthy organization will realize that not all team members will like each other or become friends outside of the work environment. They will, although, learn to respect each other and recognize each member's value in achieving the greater macro objective of the organization. It is part of the leader's duties to remind the employee of this aspect of respect and collaboration constantly. Remember that human nature is very selfish, and this will create dynamics of individuals vying for control and/or power over others or processes. A culture of respect and collaboration needs to be established by each and every leader. Lead by example and eliminate all internal conflict immediately.

Within smaller organizations it is very healthy to have the ability to cross train individuals.

Prior to the October Financial crisis of 2008 Iberia Tiles had reached a total employee count of 120 individuals. We were present in five different physical locations in the U.S. and also had commercial offices in Panama and the Caribbean. During our growth in the early part of the decade we had some foresight to cross-train our team members, but by the time the 2004 construction boom impacted us we were grasping at straws to keep up with the business volume and abandoned the cross-training. From 2008 to 2012 we were forced to close three locations and lay off over 80 individuals. By 2012 we were down to 20 employees and once again forced to cross-train out of necessity. My point to you is that based on the experience of 2008, we really never know what type of external conditions will impact our organization and it is best to be prepared for the worst-case scenario while hoping and working toward the most perfect scenario. I would suggest that you have one back-up individual trained for every single permanent position so that if you lose the individual unexpectedly the organization will not suffer.

Tip 20. Spend time building your team.

Tip 21. Spend time with your new candidate.

Tip 22. Establish a list of items the candidate needs to learn and who will train them.

Tip 23. Establish a creed to share with all team members.

Tip 24. Establish Core Values by which the organization will live.

Tip 25. Establish codes of conduct and dress that create uniformity.

Tip 26. Have the employee sign the Employee Handbook for file.

Tip 27. Have the entire team participate in the new employee training.

Tip 28. Establish cross training for important positions for future longevity.

Regardless of whether you are taking on a new leadership position or whether you have grown into a leadership position, there is a certain amount of pressure that you will feel. This pressure, or stress, will typically be both internal and external. Internally you will want to fill your obligations and perform to the expectations you have set for yourself. Externally you will want to do good by those who have empowered you to lead the way. You will undoubtedly want to fulfill the expectations of those whom you are leading and most probably have certain fears regarding how you will perform. These fears are unavoidable for responsible human beings. The way you deal with these fears is what will separate the good from the great no matter whether you have been elected the President of the United States of America or whether you are elected as your Fraternity President. As long as you believe in yourself and treat others with humility, you will find that you will fulfill much more than the internal and external expectations set. I personally will be eternally grateful to Fernando Vila and Rosa Sugrañes for the myriad of leadership opportunities they helped me assume during my early career years at Iberia Tiles. Until this day I can remember the fears and anxieties that I faced with each and every opportunity. Fortunately, along with the opportunities, I also was provided with some of the tools with which I was able to confront my day to day obligations. The tools that I was not provided, I sought out. Many of these tools have been described within this section and I hope that one day they might be helpful to you.

CHAPTER TWO:

LISTENING

Most great team builders are great COMMUNICATORS! Good communication is not always necessary, but it sure helps increase the clarity and vision for the organizations surrounding their leaders. There are many different forms and styles of communication. Each one of us has to find the form that works best for us and for the people within our organization. As leaders, we are required to manage perceptions and expectations while we set agendas and visions for the entities we lead. This is one of the most daunting challenges we face as leaders. One very basic premise of good communication is being capable of listening. Make sure that your team has access and ways to communicate their desires, fears, needs, and wants. It is fundamental for people on our teams to feel a sense of engagement and contribution. Most people want to make a difference. Most of them want to make a difference for an organization that also makes a difference and praises those who do so. Make sure you schedule opportunities to listen to your team members. When listening to them, do so with your eyes and ears, and acknowledge their contributions. Always treat the people who surround you with respect. They in turn will respect you.

Listening to your team members is a crucial part of success. Most of your team members are the experts of their particular field at that particular time. They are in the trenches and are living experiences that are difficult for most leaders to experience in the same fashion. Most definitely, larger organizations with more layers of management will experience this issue much worse than smaller organizations. It is our job as leaders to listen to our team members and provide them with the necessary tools to act upon their suggestions. Once we do this continuously and successfully, we will create an environment of collaboration and personal responsibility which achieves an "outside-in" management approach vs. an "inside-out" management approach. In other words: I listen to the market and to my team members and act upon what they tell me = "outside-in" vs. I decide what the organization is going to do and communicate it to my team and to the market = "inside-out". Some organizations are forced to be more "inside-out" than others due to their resources. But even the most "inside-out" companies need to listen to the market to ensure greater potential of success with their products or services. "Inside-out" companies are forced to spend more time and money creating market demands for their products vs. those companies that are "outside-in" providing the goods and services that the market has requested and will therefore demand with less exposure.

Listening is also part of the motivation process. I would suggest you understand the difference between scheduled and non-scheduled listening so that your team can also understand the rules of engagement in order to achieve efficient processes. Time management is one of the most important facets that professionals need to learn.

At the age of 22, I had completed two years of logistics, purchasing, customer service, and sales training at Iberia Tiles. During this time I worked many hours and enjoyed every single component of each job. Due to my efforts and comprehension I was requested by our CEO to assume the Purchasing Manager role. The position had become un-expectantly vacant and I was the best solution at the time. I considered it lucky to be promoted to such a position with great responsibility at such an early age. Our CEO later explained that his grandfather did not believe in luck but defined luck as being when preparation meets an opportunity. I was prepared to seize an opportunity that was presented to me.

At the time, the Purchasing Manager's role was essentially responsible for over-seeing a $3,000,000 product investment and ensuring 120 turn and earns by an almost just in time replenishment system while making sure that back-orders did not increase. We had 30 sales representatives and were selling tiles and stones in four different geographical markets. We had recently signed on to become one of Home Depot's Expo Design Center's first tile suppliers. We carried over 3,000 stock keeping units and had an additional 3,000 or more available via special orders with over 60 suppliers in Spain, Italy, Turkey, Dominican Republic, and Brazil. Needless to say, I was very busy and it was a daunting task. I held the Purchasing Manager role for two years and learned a lot. In retrospect, now I realize that one of the first lessons I learned that would stay with me for always is how to listen.

Being new to the position, I quickly realized that my success would be determined by my ability to listen and learn from others. I needed to listen to our salespeople and clients regarding new products. I needed to listen to our vendors regarding industry trends. I needed to listen to our management team to understand our financial and logistical capacity needs. At the same time I had to learn on how to limit and filter my listening so that I would not allow others to occupy my time.

Over the first four months, my day would start at 7:30 a.m. and end at 11p.m. Needless to say, it was an exhausting period. During the regular business hours I would spend my time on the phone with vendors and sales associates. My day of inventory analysis and replenishment reviews would start after 6 p.m. I soon realized that something needed to change. The situation I was in was unsustainable long term. With the help of our CEO, I decided to track each and every phone call by recording the person calling, purpose of call, and result. I was receiving an extra-ordinary amount of calls about the same primary issues: stock availability, lead times, and technical data. I also was receiving an extraordinary amount of phone calls to answer questions that I should not have to be answering. Being customer service oriented, I had not learned how to say "no" to anyone, and it was very fulfilling to me to feel needed by others. Unfortunately the combination of the phone calls and long hours were taking their toll physically and I had to do something to control my own time. Therefore I learned to filter. First, we created a database of technical data that could be sourced by all employees at any given time. Secondly, we updated all incoming order and stock information so that the necessary audience could check statuses without having to pick up the phone. Thirdly, we started a zero phone call campaign to encourage the entire organization to think about working more efficiently, as well as thinking before asking. During the first few weeks of starting these initiatives people would still contact me for answers that were available in the system. It is human nature for people to seek the paths of least resistance and find easy solutions that require smaller individual efforts. For many of our team members, this meant picking up the phone and asking me to provide the answers they needed. Other individuals got the message immediately and were very content to have information at their fingertips and become more independent. For the less independent members I implemented a three-call rule. During the first call I explained the new tools at their disposal and gave them the answer they were seeking. During the second phone call for the same information I would once again explain how to use the resources at their disposal, however, I did not give them the answer so that they would have to find it on their own. The third time they called for the same information I kindly informed them that I could not provide the answer and they would have to find it on their own. Within two months the majority of the organization was working more efficiently, and I was able to reduce the dedication of my time answering calls two to three hours a day and dedicate the balance of my time to reordering stock and planning. My day became much shorter, and I was much happier with my results. There were always one or two individuals who tried to utilize my time vs. theirs, and I continued to try to coach them to become more independent. They were great sales associates with a skill base that made it harder for them to cope with the new system, and I was flexible enough to assist them over the years.

Filtering information is important not only for time management, but it is also important to consider that not all individuals think alike or have similar perspectives. All perspectives are valid in a free speech environment as long as the opinions expressed do not violate the rights of the other individuals. The book titled <u>The One Minute Manager</u> by Kenneth Blanchard and Spencer Johnson published in 1982 discusses the fact that people want to be listened to. The premise of the book, as the title suggests, is that it only requires one minute for a manager to spend with their team in order to allow them to express their needs, desires, and objectives that will help move the organization forward. The objective is to have people mange themselves by establishing clear goals that can be followed. Constructive feedback or immediate reprimands of negative behavior help keep everyone on target. I have always been a big believer of goal setting. Some see it as a waste of time. If and when it is done efficiently, goal setting can have a very powerful impact on the organization. I suggest that goals be set by the General Management and Ownership to set the tone for the organization. I suggest they be set at each department level to clarify the team goals. Additionally, each individual should also set goals. Once the organization is accustomed to the goal setting process, they will do it quickly and keep on target.

When setting goals it is important that they be **BAITED**. My Dad loves fishing. One of the lessons I have learned from fishing with him is that using the appropriate bait is crucial to success. Keeping the word **BAIT** in mind also will help your goal setting process.

Goals should be:

Benchmarked – Measurable

Actual - Relevant to the current environment

Important - Impacting the bottom line

Timely - Achievable in well-defined time frame

Easy or **E**normous - Achievable (small or short-term) goals will help motivate the team; while larger goals will help increase results. They should be one or the other, but always have a certain percentage for the ability to succeed so that they are relevant.

Detailed - Well-defined in understandable terms

Having measurable goals is crucial for us to know where we stand. Think about trying to lose 10 pounds without a scale. You probably can *guestimate* your progress based on other factors but it is almost impossible for you to know if you have reached or exceeded the goal with certainty without a scale. Business goals are the same. If they are not measurable, they are not good goals.

The goals should also be actual and relevant to the current environment in which you are working. Selling $20,000,000 per year at Iberia Tiles was very doable in 2006. By 2009 the environment had changed and we were fortunate to reach $16,000,000. Your team members and customers will help you understand the actuality of your organization within the market. It is important for you to LISTEN to them so that you can help set goals that are relevant.

All goals should be important in terms of impacting the bottom line. If not directly impacting bottom line, they should at least impact the Value Incentive Service Added (VISA) proposition which will ultimately help the bottom line. The VISA concept is very important to an organization and will be developed more within the second part of the book. In summary, every organization, every team member, every salesperson need to focus on creating their own VISA= Value Incentive Service Added. In other words: everyone needs to focus on communicating what makes them special. We all have different perspectives of what creates added value. For example: There are TV Remote Controllers that will perform a million functions. If the consumer only wants a remote that changes channels and volume it is likely that they will not appreciate (value) the increased cost associated with creating a remote with many other functions. The same happens with organizations and team members. We each have to find a way to create added values for our clients and organizations so that we can help secure our positions within the marketplace. Occasionally the goals that we establish will impact the VISA of the organization if and when they are not impacting the bottom line. The best example I can use to help you understand this point is having you imagine a retail store manager's goals. A retail store manager's number one goal should be to generate the sales revenue levels needed by the organization. This is obvious. It is possible that within certain periods of time they will need to dedicate their time to other things that do not directly impact this objective. Going through a six month store remodeling process could be one of these goals. Remodeling a retail store does not necessarily impact the sales positively. A remodeled and refreshed store does, although, directly impact the VISA if done properly. The perception of the market when visiting the store will be new and fresh which will hopefully help the store increase sales and retain market share in the long run and therefore impacting the bottom line. Unfortunately it is not always the case and stores are merely remodeled enhancing the buying experience without directly impacting the bottom line. Despite this, remodeling a store still can be a very important goal for a retail store manager to oversee if part of the master organizational plan and previously approved by his/her superiors.

If goals are not timely, they have lesser chances of being accomplished. Timeliness helps elevate the urgency. It is preferable to set goals with monthly, quarterly, or yearly time objectives. It is easy to lose track or become distracted from goals with longer time objectives. Creating a time objective for goals also helps us organize our time efficiently so that we can accomplish the various objectives that we have in mind. To this point it is not uncommon for goals to have sub-goals or action items, as I call them, which are designed to help you ultimately achieve the broader goal.

Goals can be Easy or Enormous (Achievable or Audacious). I like setting easy goals that are Achievable so that it creates a sense of success and accomplishment by the team. At the same time I can have in mind and discuss an enormous goal that we would like to be able to achieve in the future. Enormous goals help us dream and strive for higher levels of performance.

Last but not least, goals should be detailed. If goals are not specific they will not be understood by the parties directly impacted by the goals. Vague goals leave too much room for interpretation and excuses if not accomplished. There is a big difference between having a goal to increase revenues vs. a more detailed goal of adding two new customers who will purchase $50,000 per year each. The objectives are the same but one is vague and the other is specific.

At the General Manager and Ownership level, I recommend that the organization spend anywhere from a weekend to a week prior to the fiscal year budgeting process to set the company's goals. Rolling five year strategic goals can be very important for stable companies in stable markets. For less stable organizations in volatile markets it can be difficult to follow five year plans. At the very least it is important for the top leaders to establish some sort of longer term vision that the organization will work towards. Using a moderator can be very helpful to conduct these strategic sessions efficiently. Time for brainstorming and open constructive discussions is very helpful. Ultimately someone needs to be responsible for writing down and establishing the conclusions achieved. These goals will be used as the framework for the General Manager to implement with his/her team. These goals can be reviewed annually or bi-annually depending on the dynamics of the organization. Goals that are not followed and reviewed periodically are generally not worth the paper they are written on.

At a departmental level it is possible to set goals in one day or half-day sessions. These goals will follow the general goals set by the top management but will be more specific to what each department needs to achieve. For operational departments the goals could focus on service commitments desired. They can also be efficiency-oriented. Sales departments can focus on market share and value added initiatives. Administrative departments can focus on key indicators or reporting efficiencies that will help advance the organization's achievements. These goals should be reviewed at least quarterly.

Individual goals can be set in much shorter sessions. They also can be reviewed monthly or weekly, depending on the timeliness of the desired accomplishments. These goals should also be part of the individual evaluation review process. Individuals that consistently achieve goals should be praised while those that consistently fall short should find ways to remedy results and/or deal with failure.

Setting a tone of success along with a reward/penalty culture will help establish a culture of success and personal responsibility.

All levels of goal setting should be inclusive to the participants and therefore part of the listening process. Great individuals will have clear ideas of what they need to achieve and how to go about reaching their objectives. It is up to the manager to learn how to "obey" and follow what the team members are suggesting by being supportive and providing the necessary tools that they will need from the organization. Providing direction is part of these tools as managers cannot blindly allow their team members to do what they want to do when they want to do it. Everything must be in context and the manager is responsible for providing this direction.

Tip 29. Learn how to listen with your eyes and ears.

Tip 30. Schedule time for listening to your team.

Tip 31. Manage your time efficiently.

Tip 32. Learn how to say no to the things that might distract you.

Tip 33. Identify information sharing systems to help communication efficiency.

Tip 34. Dedicate time to train your team members so that they can become autonomous.

Tip 35. Mange the Listening process by setting goals.

Tip 36. Set BAITED goals.

In order to lead, one must listen and obey! Listening to our team members is crucial to the success of any organization. Listening to our customers is equally important. Both our employees and customers will tell us exactly what we need to do and how we need to do it. Goal setting, as described previously is one way to organize this function. Another classical method that also can be used to listen is the common SWOT (Strengths, Weaknesses, Opportunities, Threats) Analysis. This method has been taught in managerial courses since the 1960's and is one that has personally worked for me and many other organizations.

The SWOT Analysis provides an opportunity for the organization's teams to write down the strengths and weaknesses of the company. The objective is to maximize the strengths and minimize the weaknesses. The opportunities and threats are generally market driven forces. The customer's input is very valuable in determining the opportunities that the market is providing. I recommend that the SWOT Analysis not only be done on your own company but also on the companies you consider your competition. This will help you and your team devise the appropriate strategic plans to help insure your place and growth within the market.

Tip 37. Listen to your customers.

Tip 38. Perform regular SWOT Analysis on your organization as well as competing companies

CHAPTER THREE:
OBEYING=ACTION

Obeying requires action. The most brilliant strategic ideas will be useless if they are not carried out with the proper action. Activity is required by the entire organization, but most importantly by the top management. Behavior and actions of organizations will typically emulate the behavior and actions of their leaders. For this reason it is important to create a leadership team that has a balanced skill set. These skills will complement strengths and weaknesses as no single person is perfect. It is important for us to recognize our individual strengths and weaknesses in order to make sure that we are conduits to the appropriate balance. Recognizing our own strengths is usually very easy. Recognizing our weaknesses is a little more challenging, but necessary. Complementing our weaknesses is crucial in achieving success. Obeying represents the ability to be humble enough to follow direction given by others. Leaders that are able to visualize and act upon the direction created by their team members in the trenches will be more successful than the traditional models whereby the leaders expect their "subjects" to follow a "blind obedience" concept used by many militaries. The point of obedience is not necessarily to be on time. It is to do the right thing at the right time. Our team members are able to help us understand the right thing at the right time.

Most religious rites have a common thread in the fact that we are submissive to a higher being. Those who have embraced this concept will find it easier to obey and act upon the direction of others. Our legal system also helps us with this concept. Laws are implemented to help the greater community live in harmony. Some of us find it easy to follow direction. Others struggle with this concept as they continuously seek to exert their own will and self-satisfaction. Those of us with great role models during our development years will find it easier than those of us with bad role models. Ultimately obeying can be a decision that an individual makes no matter what the situation or background. It is an attitude and state of mind.

There are some practical steps that we can take to help us obey and take action upon direction given by others. The first step is being capable of listening as discussed in the previous section of this book. Once we listen and have a clear idea of the direction to be taken we must find ways to act upon the direction. Goal setting as discussed in the previous chapter is part of this process. The goals become action items to be followed.

Another great practical tool to help us obey and create action items for ourselves and others is writing things down. Writing is a great form of communication and is a great way to create clarity and permanence. It is impossible for us to remember one hundred percent of everything that we encounter daily. Early during my career I was fortunate to work with a very successful and wise Account Manager named George Grubisa. I was six months into my management training program at the Iberia Tiles Pompano Beach branch and George was one of four outside Account Managers. I was performing my customer service training module along with one other representative. Our job was basically to support the outside sales initiatives by working from the customer service counter where clients would come to pick up orders or call them in. George gave me a notebook and direction. He suggested that I write everything down in the bounded notebook. This way I would never forget or lose an action item. I obeyed this direction and embraced it as part of my own. On a daily basis I wrote down and checked off each action item that I had completed. I reviewed those that were pending for completion and made sure that I never left any behind. I found this exercise so useful that I kept these notebooks throughout my tenure at Iberia Tiles and gave every new employee that I hired the same bounded notebook with the same instructions.

Most of the team members embraced this concept better than others but all of them found it useful to help them keep track of their action items. Once we become leaders, we are no longer measured by our individual performance but are measured by the performance of the entire division which we manage. Part of being a professional manager is being able to motivate others to do what you want them to do without them necessarily feeling that you are doing so. Having a clear and written method of following up on action items is a helpful part of this process.

Another very efficient form of written communications that help us obey action items are e-mails and texts. They efficiently allow groups of individuals to help generate ideas and action items for each other. They are very powerful tools that have definitely made us more efficient. I highly encourage you to use them without losing sight of the value of a verbal conversation, or face-to-face meeting. There is a time and place for both. There is a saying in Spanish that I love and use often, "hablando se entiende la gente" which means "by speaking with each other, people, understand each other". Generally speaking it is best to communicate sensitive issues verbally as it allows us to modify our tone and message based on the others' reactions. How many times have you sent an email that has been mis-interpreted or read out of context? The same will happen to others writing to you. Never be quick to judge or jump to conclusions. Think things through carefully and verbally clarify any misunderstandings. Never write to others when angry or sad. These are very personal feelings that can deeply impact the party receiving your message. Share them sparingly and with a clear objective in mind.

Tip 39. Learn how to obey by being humble and respectful of others.

Tip 40. Obey by taking action.

Tip 41. Obey by helping create action for others.

Tip 42. Practice time management.

Tip 43. Learn to act efficiently with written skills.

Tip 44. Know when to write or communicate verbally.

Tip 45. Managers are measured by the results of their team members, not individually.

Another form of obeying and creating action items is by the use of efficient meetings.

I am a big proponent of efficient meetings. I am a big opponent of disruptive meetings. Meetings are necessary for most organizations and very effective with the right leader and right team. Meetings should have a purpose. They should also follow an agenda. There will be many times that a well conducted meeting does not impact every single participant. It is also possible that some of the meeting participants will try to sabotage the meeting or impact the content negatively out of rebellion. The meeting leader should be ready to deal with these individuals in a delicate way. I recommend conducting meetings when a large majority (70-80%) has a positive take away from meeting. Meetings can be very generic or very specific. They should always have a clear agenda with a specific time-frame. The shorter the better. Make sure the environment is not boring or conducive to napping. Stand up often if durations are long. Make sure that people understand that their mobile devices should be set aside during the duration of the meeting.

Meetings should often be inclusive of as many of the team members for which the subject is intended. They should be controlled so that they do not becoming complaining sessions. The leader should keep the group on-topic and delicately find ways to "side-bar" topics that are important but need to be addressed in other meetings or conversations. Most meetings should generate a list of action items with responsible individuals to execute in later hours, days, weeks or months. Plan to address these action items in subsequent settings to ensure that there is continuity and commitment of accomplishment. Organizations that are run as democracies do not usually create the results necessary in today's environment. It is important to seek other's input and ideas, but ultimately there needs to be a decision maker who will be accountable. I like the term of "Benevolent Dictator" used to describe certain historical leaders, without getting into the politics of the negative connotation of Dictatorships. I relate this term to an organization in the sense that ultimately a leader needs to make decisions for the organization which he/she is accountable. Great leaders are able to get the majority of the team/organization behind the ideas so that there is a sense of commonality. On some occasions the leader will have to embrace ideas that go against his/her own personal thoughts based on the fact that the majority of the team is engaged in making them happen. This is part of the obeying process. Once the leader decides to accept the idea proposed it is important for him/her to "own" the idea as his/her own. There is no room for excuses or doubt. On occasion the contrary also will happen when leaders have a vision that is contrary to popular belief. It is the job of the leader to rally the troops and make sure that the team will at least try the new concept and that the possibility of sabotage is minimal along the way. There will ALMOST ALWAYS be someone that wants the new vision to fail. It is important to identify these individuals and keep them motivated along the way. This is part of creating a culture of obedience.

Tip 46. Learn how to run an efficient meeting.
a. Set an agenda with a limited meeting time and stick to it.
b. Be inclusive of participants.
c. Do not let the meeting become a complaining session.
d. Find a way to "side-bar" important issues that arise and are necessary to deal with during a later time.
e. Create list of action items with responsible parties to execute.
f. Follow up on the action items.
g. Find a way to become a Benevolent Leader without becoming a Democratic Bureaucracy.

With today's technology it is very possible to execute many different action items and visions via e-mail and remote conferencing. E-mails have replaced the need for the past "corporate" memos which still have their place. Finding a way to manage e-mails is a very important topic that can be dealt with separately, but here are some basic suggestions. Always think about what you write. This might sound a little paranoid, but it is very wise advice in today's litigious environment.

Writing leaves permanent records, and, with today's technology, will follow you for good or for bad for the rest of your lives. It is quite often that I have seen team members get into e-mail squabbles.

Occasionally, I have seen team members and clients send heated messages that should not have been written. On one occasion, I personally wanted to modify the behavior of one of my best salespeople and wrote a memo to explain the desired behavior and obstacles. The salesperson took the memo in a very bad way (rightfully so), and from then on, I learned my lesson regarding memos. Once you have thought through your message it is always a good idea to have someone review your written communications. There are many times that we overlook errors or make common mistakes of interpretation. (This book has been reviewed by three different individuals for accuracy. We apologize beforehand for any errors found within.) It is much better for someone with an objective outlook to help provide a second opinion. It is obviously impossible for us to do this for every single communication. Most of us have good basic educations that will allow us to minimize our errors and make ourselves understood. I typically use a second set of eyes for documents of significant importance or longevity. Procedural Memos, Employee Handbooks, Educational Memos, Global Client Communications, to name a few, are some of the types of documents I always have a second set of eyes review. The only exception to this rule applies to grammatical mistakes. NEVER send anything in writing with grammatical mistakes. Use your spell checks and translators if you are weak in certain grammatical aspects. Seek help from others, and, last but not least, have a disclaimer on your communication that there may be grammatical mistakes if you have no other option. People judge us by our actions and on many occasions, I have seen many clients, friends, and/or colleagues reach erroneous conclusions regarding individuals based on their poor written communications. People are very judgmental by nature and this we cannot control. We can, however, control our communications. Keep your written communications short and simple and to the point.

Tip 47. Find a way to use effective written communications.

a. Think about what you write, re-read what you have

written, and use Spell-check before sending.

b. Think about the objective of your communication.

c. Think about the state of mind of the receiving party.

d. Perception becomes reality and many things are open to interpretation. Be aware of how the receiving party will interpret your communication.

e. Assume that common sense is the least common of senses.

f. Have an objective set of eyes review important communications.

g. Always avoid grammatical errors.

h. Keep written communications short, simple, and pointed.

i. Make sure your objective is clearly accomplished.

As usual, obedience also creates the opportunity for disobedience. Another very important attribute to great leaders and team builders is the ability to DEAL WITH CONFLICT. Unfortunately we live in a conflictive world. Most of the civilized societies are fortunate to have established certain "rules of engagement" by which we can conduct our lives with minimal physical conflict. We will always have to deal with conflictive ways of thinking and/or ideals, being that we are free-willed individuals with the ability to have our own thoughts and make our own decisions with minimal interference. The amount of liberty we have varies from nation to nation and from government to government. For the purposes of this book I will address conflicts that I have experienced during the regular business cycle, or socially.

It is understandable that larger organizations have more potential for conflict due to increased variability between individuals. This is not always the case, as I have also seen a large amount of conflict in smaller organizations due to the attitude of one or two individuals. These negative individuals can be highly toxic and contagious to the rest of the organization. Great leaders are able to identify this risk and deal with it immediately. I always encourage reconciliation as the first step. Excellent individuals are hard to find and occasionally excellent performers can be conflictive. It is important to try and identify the cause of the conflict and work toward resolution with the individual in a very short period of time (one week maximum). If behavior is not modified within one week it is absolutely necessary to eliminate the toxic behavior by eliminating the individual. In most cases this is easier said than done due to regulatory labor laws and lack of replacements. The labor laws are necessary and need to be followed. We should never allow toxic behavior due to a lack of replacement, as we should always have three replacements identified for every position we manage and be constantly recruiting, if not the case. There are some occasions where the individual cannot be immediately eliminated due to lack of replacement and the void created by doing so is more damaging than the toxic behavior. During these occasions you must have an objective and patient outlook by finding the correct timely replacement and dealing with the individual when the time is right. Do not let too much time pass you by as the negative effect upon your organization will grow exponentially.

It is important to deal with conflict in an objective and pro-active manner. Unacceptable behaviors should also be addressed in a timely manner. It is best to try to deal with conflictive behavior in a setting which does not further impact the organization. I have personally found that dealing with this type of behavior in private settings has worked for me. During this time it is important to set aside personal emotions and prejudices by dealing with the objective issue and offering the conflictive individual a path of reconciliation, if possible. Very clear standards of behavior should be set and followed fairly with every individual. It is possible to do this in a pro-active and positive manner so that the result of the resolution is not de-motivating to the individual. Further de-motivation and/or negativity can create further conflict and create rebellion which will result in increased unacceptable behavior, which sometimes is manifested privately in a stealth-like manner. Organizations dealing with restrictive labor laws will have to implement a warning system which allows documentation of the employee's behavior in the event of possible future separation from the organization. The legal implementations of dealing with conflictive conduct should also be considered when implementing this process. I always recommend that your team be clear on what is not acceptable so that there is never an element of surprise in the event of future firing. The organization I was part of during most of my career followed three strikes and you are out type guideline whereby we would give a verbal warning at the first sign of conflict, which was later escalated to a written warning, and ultimately firing if the problem continued. This process can also be followed when dealing with lack of job performance or incompetence. No matter what the case, it is always best to find a diplomatic way to address the matter. I suggest that if you ever feel that the behavior needs to be addressed with harsher actions you consider the possibility of immediately separating from the individual as it is likely that the harsh approach will lead to dissent and eventual separation sooner or later. This can impact the organization negatively and should be avoided. By the same token, not addressing a negative behavior or conflict in a timely manner will send a message to the entire organization that this type of behavior is tolerable. This apathetic behavior will eventually lead to conduct that is deeply rooted within the organization and very difficult to remedy.

Hiring and firing individuals is part of a leader's obligations. Hiring and individual is not easy but usually very rewarding (at least at the beginning). Firing an individual is typically not so rewarding. Even when the individual is very conflictive and it is clear that the best result for the organization and the individual will be his or her separation, most people have a hard time with the firing process and rightfully so. For this reason I will divert from the obedience theme and give the reader a couple of tips that will help him/her with the firing process. **Disclaimer:** These are tips that have been developed over twenty years of management and have generally worked for me. Human Resources management is a very subjective issue and much will depend on the circumstances of the firing. When in doubt please check with a Human Resource professional or attorney so that the appropriate advice is given for the appropriate situation.

Tip 48. Remember that we are all human beings with emotions. It is ok to be humane when letting someone go. There is away to be humane without becoming emotionally attached.

Tip 49. "When the going gets tough, the tough get going" We are leaders, and as leaders we are responsible for making the tough calls objectively. Business is business and our obligations as leaders are to the business.

Tip 50. It is best if the person being let go is not blind-sided by the reality. Establish the expectations of performance at the beginning of the candidate's employment. If being let go for cause (lack of performance or negligence), hopefully the candidate will remember the performance expectation and realize that they are not being met. Typically warnings can be issued prior to the firing. If someone is being let go due to lay-offs or reorganization the team member will often know that this possibility is at hand.

Tip 51. Be sincere, clear, and honest when communicating the reasons of separation as long as the truth is not insulting, demoralizing, or offending.

Tip 52. Be empathetic to the individual being let go without becoming emotionally attached.

Tip 53. When in doubt, consult a Human Resources Professional or Attorney.

Previously, I was discussing the importance of managing conflict as part of the leadership and obedience section. Creating a well-defined corporate culture is crucial to this objective and also will help with the firing process. Defining a corporate culture is directly correlated to creating a well defined- mission statement. The corporate culture that leadership is able to establish will define the behavior of the organization. This well defined culture will be greater than the possible impact any one person or group of individuals can have within the organization. For example, if an organization makes health and fitness as part of their culture you will find that team members will quickly become obsessed with making it part of their lifestyle. The lifestyle becomes contagious and the individual or groups of individuals that continue smoking and bringing fattening doughnuts to the office will not be able to dent the determination of the group. It is crucial that the leaders of the organization embrace, live, and believe in the corporate culture to ensure that it is maintained and defined as the organization evolves with the market.

There are many good examples of organizations both small and large that have developed a well-defined culture which permeates throughout the individuals. This culture can also become a competitive advantage or disadvantage depending on how it is perceived in the marketplace.

Tip 54. Learn to deal with conflict.

    a. Reconcile toxic behavior or eliminate causes quickly.

    b. Establish clear rules of conduct.

    c. Deal with individuals privately.

    d. Be pro-active and timely.

    e. Be diplomatic and motivating during the reconciliation.

    f. Avoid harsh encounters or punishments as they can create more negativity.

    g. Do not let conflict go un-addressed.

    h. Set a positive corporate culture that is larger than any individual behavior.

An important part of creating a positive corporate culture is by having a great vision. Great leaders are typically also great VISIONARIES. Creating a vision involves obeying your instinct, as well as the recommendations of those who surround you. In my experience there are two types of visionaries:

1. The person or entrepreneur who has a vision to start the business.
2. The person who is able to embrace the vision and grow it.

As mentioned previously, we all have our strengths and weaknesses. There are countless case studies that portray entrepreneurs who have a vision to bring a certain service or product to the market. Many of the major successful companies that we know today started in this fashion i.e., Ford, Apple, Microsoft, Wal-Mart, The Oprah Winfrey Show, and many more Once the vision and passion for a product and service is created comes the need and ability to scale the product and service to a larger market. I have had the benefit to work both forms of visions. The first was co-creating with my wife and brother-in-law, a company called Piscisecure, dedicated to the pool fence safety industry in Alabama and Spain. The second, while at Iberia Tiles, was by embracing the vision held by the founders in 1979. Both types of visions are necessary for the success of organizations. The entrepreneurial vision helps create a product or service that is needed in a market due to a niche or demand that is not being addressed. The managerial vision helps define purpose for the team members who will help the organization carry out its objectives.

During my tenure at Iberia Tiles, I was fortunate to embrace a great vision held by the Sugrañes family. Once I embraced this vision and made it my own, I was able to help grow the vision within the markets in which we were operating. During this process we developed what we called the "Iberia Way". It was nothing more than a document that recorded the corporate culture and customer service cycle we expected to live by. There is a great book called SECRET SERVICE, written by John R. Dijulios III, which I highly recommend. Within the book you will find examples of well-known companies that were able to create a customer service cycle that eventually became their Value Influenced Service Added (VISA) in the market. Creating your VISA within your particular organization and industry is fundamental to your long-term success. Creating a VISA for managers and sales representatives is also key. In aforementioned book you will be able to identify the companies mentioned, as well as the traits that have eventually defined them. You would like to eventually be able to create this value added cycle within your organization without much effort. The behaviors defined in this cycle become habitual to the team members and eventually form part of your culture. Creating this vision is fundamental as it will separate you from your competition and should be powerful enough to keep your customer base engaged and loyal.

Studies have shown that a high percentage of customers are lost due to attitudes of indifference by one or more individuals within the organization. Customers expect companies to obey their desires. Part of creating a customer service cycle is ensuring that every single team member is on point and committed to delivering what is expected by the customer. Within retail environments it is fundamental to spend time and attention on the actual store and ordering experience. It is almost common sense to expect products to be well displayed and have competent people tending to the customer needs. Most organizations do quite well with this part of the cycle. Eventually the products or services need to be delivered. This is where many organizations have room for improvement as they do not spend the same amount of time ensuring that the logistics and delivery channels accompany the retail and sales experience. Imagine a beautiful and expensive furniture store that delays every single delivery. Under such circumstances, it will not take long for the customer base to erode and for the customers to find other sources that provide a comparable product in a timely manner. Make sure that you are able to create your own VISA and help communicate the vision to your organization on a consistent basis.

Tip 55. Create and communicate your vision continuously.

Tip 56. Create and communicate your VISA within your organization and market.

Tip 57. Obey your customers!

Obeying in business is equivalent to taking action. We must listen to our clients, employees, and bosses and follow their direction. Setting goals and learning to effectively communicate and run efficient meetings is part of this process.

CHAPTER FOUR:

LEADING CONCLUSION

The demands of today's marketplace are great. Being a professional manager requires diligence and preparation both at a professional and personal level. Having spent a large amount of my youth in Spain I am very connected to its culture and way of living. It is acknowledged by most people who understand the Spanish culture that most professionals "work to live" whereas in the U.S. we "live to work". At the end of the day, it is necessary for most of us to dedicate a large portion of our day to productive activity in order to be able to generate enough income for our personal needs. Being able to dedicate this time to something that we enjoy is fundamental. Doing this with a positive and humble attitude will help us achieve much satisfaction. Having a positive impact on the people that surround us is very important. Living a balanced lifestyle which combines both professional and personal satisfaction will help us keep our motivation for the achievement of our goals.

Leadership is something that we will all be called to do at some point within our lifetime. Listening to those that surround us and obeying their direction will help us lead with fulfillment and success. One of my favorite teachings is more than three thousand years old and was recorded by King Solomon who is considered to be a wise leader and profit by the Christian, Jewish, and Muslim traditions alike, is found within the old testament book of Proverbs. The King James Version of Proverbs, Chapter 1 verse 5 reads as follows: "A wise man will hear and will increase learning: and a man of understanding shall attain unto wise counsels." The concept of being a wise leader by listening and obeying is not new. It has been with us for thousands of years.

Hopefully the previous chapters of this book have helped define some practical steps to leading by listening and obeying. Hopefully I have done so by providing well organized ideas and insights to A) Living a Balanced Lifestyle, B) Teambuilding, C) Goal Setting, D) Communicating, and E) Vision Creating. These practical tips have worked for me over the last twenty years. Implementing these steps will require a personal choice on your part. They also will require effort. Paper easily records the most brilliant of theories. Only in their implementation do they become useful. My sincerest desire is that one or more of my tips can be implemented successfully by you.

Last but not least, I encourage you to become an All Star! Do so by sharing your success, knowledge, and love with others. We are part of a universal world that is full of people that are less fortunate than we. I became an After School All Star five years ago by invitation of a great friend. The After School All Stars organization is a not-for-profit that offers a free afterschool program for youth in middle school grades. The program was started by Governor Schwarzenegger in California when he saw a need that "at risk" neighborhood middle-school age kids have for after school care. Within Miami-Dade County we have been able to run programs in up to 34 schools serving over 2,000 kids. Nationally we have been able to accomplish much more. There has been nothing more rewarding for me than to be able to help people in need of help. I highly encourage that you do the same whether it be through your church or another charitable organization like After School All Stars. Sharing your time, talent, and treasure with others will be an investment you will never regret and will be sure to receive compounded returns on investment that cannot be equaled!

PART II:
SELLING BY LISTENING AND OBEYING

Selling is one of the most important functions that any organization can perform. The selling function creates the necessary revenue stream for most organizations to operate. There are very few industries or companies that do not require some level of sales and/or customer support. The next few chapters will focus on twenty years of selling experience within the ceramic tile and marble industry at a retail and wholesale level. There are many components of this experience that can be used for any industry. All of them are very relevant for any distribution or manufacturing entity dedicated to the furnishings business.

Hopefully you have been able to read the previously written leadership section of my book so that you will be able to grasp some of the general concepts a little quicker. Most of the concepts have been developed during my twenty years of experience working and managing Iberia Tiles Corporation in Miami, Florida. Many others have been shared and embraced through many books by many different enlightened individuals on the topic of sales and customer service. Anthony Robbins is probably one of the best known sales "gurus" due to his personal marketing and exposure. His ideas are practical and easy to follow. Many other ideas have also been contributed by Jack Daly and Jerry Layo. I thank Mr. Robbins, Mr. Layo, and Mr. Daly for sharing their experience and ideas with us so that we might have an easier time carrying out our business.

Within this section I will be making the following assumptions:

1. The reader has some kind of interest or exposure to the sales activity within their organization.

2. The reader recognizes that sales activity is fundamental to development and growth of the organization. I welcome all other readers who merely have an intellectual or leadership interest in reading these sections. Hopefully they will be helpful.

CHAPTER ONE:
THE ART OF SELLING

Some of us are born with the natural talent of sales. Some of the traits that identify natural salespeople are: self-assurance, outgoing personality, positive attitude, persuasiveness, and amiability. It is possible for some of us to become very successful sales professionals without any, or at least some, of the above traits. At a basic level, sales, is essentially becoming a "mood inducer" as Anthony Robbins calls it. People enjoy being with people that they like and with whom they share common interests. People avoid people that they dislike or people that dispel negative energy. Think about the people that you personally choose to spend your free time with. What traits do they have? This process will identify the traits of a good salesman for you. We all have different interests and personalities; therefore, it is impossible for one type of sales to "fit all". This allows us to be able to identify many different types of successful sales personalities so that we can hire the correct matches for our client base. Great salespeople generate great results. It is the job of the Sales Leader to identify, recruit, hire, and train great salespeople on a constant basis. There are certain characteristics that are generally accepted as defining great salespeople.

The adjectives that describe these characteristics would be:

Amiable	Outgoing	Diligent	Happy	Friendly	Extroverted
Excited	Independent		Perseverant		Authoritative
Dependable	Strategic	Committed	Honest		Courageous

How many more can you think of? There are a number of testing tools that can help us objectively identify some of these traits. As mentioned before, I have successfully used the Predictive Index in order to help me identify some of these traits. Salespeople with these traits will typically find greater satisfaction within the job they are performing. They will often be able to generate results faster and more consistently than people without these traits.

I have stressed the importance that a positive outlook can have with performance. A positive outlook is also fundamental to the sales team. Second to attitude, I value courage and perseverance. In the following chapter we will discuss the fact that, often, sales, is a numbers game. The more we put ourselves in front of a customer, the increased chances we will have of closing a sale. We want sales associates that are courageous, as synonymous to lack of fear. Speaking to people that we do not know, and/or trying to convince others to purchase something that they may or may not need can be intimidating to a lot of people. We want to find people who are capable of breaking these barriers and will adopt "just do it" mentalities. Additionally, perseverance is required to ensure that we break these barriers on a continuous basis. Sales representatives have to become accustomed to being rejected and hearing the word "no". The representatives that are capable of recovering quickly from a negative customer encounter and moving on successfully to the next will be able to achieve faster and greater results.

There are three macro concepts to keep in mind when it comes to sales:

1. As mentioned above, great salespeople will generate great results, find them, pay them, and keep them. Bad salespeople are a waste of time. Fire them ASAP! They are bad if they do not generate results or have a bad attitude. Mediocre salespeople are the hardest to manage. They do not seem bad enough to fire but are not good enough to help the organization. Replace them ASAP!

2. Sales requires pro-activity. Managers should spend time monitoring activity. Too often we measure results. Results are

good but they do not generate future sales. Activity generates sales. Very few companies have a brand or product strong enough to fill orders like MAC.

3. You get what you inspect not what you expect! Part of motivating people is making sure they are generating results. They need small goals to help keep themselves organized, and managers should demand results.

Within the leadership chapters, I discussed the importance of identifying and recruiting great team members to help achieve the organizational objectives. Here is a refresher of the traits that we should consider when recruiting and hiring sales representatives:

1. Talent
   a. Aptitude
   b. Family background
   c. Education
2. Experience
3. Outlook = Attitude
4. Pro-activity

There are other important traits that sales successful sales representatives possess:

Engaged: The sales representative takes his/her career seriously and is dedicated to growing. They have an attitude and state of mind that allows them to absorb information like sponges. They are committed to dedicating time not only during the official workday but also afterhours so that they learn more about their business and are exposed to broader networks of potential clients. They are focused on building relationships with these clients vs. building transactions. Being engaged also means that the sales representative will be pro-active and independent which will require less management time from his/her superiors. They will understand the mission at hand and work efficiently to achieve the results needed. These individuals will show up prepared vs. others that "wing it". On a scale of 1-10, how engaged are you?

Ability to listen: As you know by now, listening is crucial to success no matter what your profession. Being able to understand and identify with others is very important. When it comes to sales it is even more important due to the fact that most of the time clients will tell us exactly what they need. All we have to do is find a solution to their need. Along with listening is the ability to ask the right questions. Successful sales representatives are capable of posing the questions that will allow them to propose a strategic proposition which will be hard to deny. This will increase the order closing potential. By the same token people that are able to listen are also comfortable with silence. Too many sales representatives "show up and throw up". They are preoccupied on how to communicate the features and values of their products/services without focusing on the need. How many questions can you think of to propose to a perspective client?

Confidence: Being confident without being arrogant is another trait common to successful sales representatives. A professional sales associate must have confidence in themselves, their service, and their organization. The sales representative is able to communicate this confidence to a potential customer. Customers will subconsciously ask, 1) "Why should I do business with you?", 2) "Why do I need your product/service?", 3) "Why should I do business with your company?" Sales representatives must be prepared to answer these kinds of questions with confidence. What are your answers?

Confidence is also what will allow a sales representative to deal with rejection. Rejection is something that most of us seek to avoid. We are programmed to seek acceptance from childhood. Confident sales representatives are able to recover quickly from rejection and move on to a new target. Confidence also will permit a sales representative to make the "ask" to a client for their business. Asking the customer to give you the business can be the difference in being successful or not.

Follow-up: You will find that most of the higher performing sales representatives are very diligent with their client and order follow-up. A high percentage of sales representatives spend a relatively small amount of time following-up with clients. Those who invest the time are able to capitalize due to the fact that the clients will appreciate the attention and service received. There are many different follow-up systems: electronic, manual, mental, etc. It is important to find the system that works for you individually. What follow up system do you use?

Reliable: Successful sales representatives are concerned about what their clients think of their service. They go about their business with high integrity and deliver more than what they promise. They are available for their clients when the clients wish to contact them. They embrace responsibility and do not hide from negative issues that might come up. This reliability will keep customers returning to the sales representative when their product or service is needed. Are you reliable?

Time management: Successful sales representatives are able to efficiently manage their time. Active sales representatives will be presented with many different opportunities that will be time-consuming. Being able to identify and focus on the ones that have higher success potential is crucial to efficient time management.

Results-Oriented: Successful sales representatives generate results. They have a no-excuse mentality and will quickly recover from failures. They are usually proud of their results as this will feed the part of their ego that drives them to continuously hunt for the "kill". Most also will appreciate the monetary rewards that accompany the sales success. They are typically more territorial and will be less team-oriented than customer service type individuals. Often, these individuals will have ambitious long-term financial goals and will have no qualms expressing them. They will view their job as a means to the end, and, as long as they are progressing toward the objective, they will remain motivated.

Successful sales representatives are able to combine their traits and use them to consistently seek revenue opportunities for the organization. They are focused on building relationships with their clients and nurturing the relationships. They are capable of becoming integrated with their customer's needs and seek ways for the organization to meet these needs. They are also capable of breaking down their macro objectives so that they can identify how to spend their daily time efficiently by focusing on activities that increase their sales success. It is the responsibility of the sales leader to keep them in front of the customer base by providing them with the necessary tools. The sales leader should focus also on building relationships with the client base so that they are not totally dependent on the sales professional. This helps create organizational consistency in the event the sales representative chooses to move on to another organization.

Sales oriented organizations must face the fact that sales alone is not sufficient. Delivering the product or service to the client is fundamental to success. For this reason, the Customer Service component of sales is crucial to the organization's viability. I encourage organizations to view their customer service representative as extensions to the sales team. Many customer service representatives become "inside" salespeople for the organization and upon occasion can forge relationships with the clients that are much deeper than the relationships forged by the sales professionals themselves.

Following this thought process, within Iberia Tiles we separated the employees into two categories: Hunters and Farmers. The Hunters were defined as the individuals that were responsible for seeking new business opportunities. The individuals called to this task were typically very motivated and outgoing. They were also very ambitious and aggressive in seeking out new opportunities. The Farmers were the individuals responsible for maintaining and nurturing the customer relationship once the Hunters were able to find them. These divisions are not meant to be black and white. There is much cross-over between Hunters and Farmers. The main point is that the organization has to realize that customer service representatives can be just as important to organizations as their sales counter parts.

Providing great customer service should be a given objective for most organizations. Unfortunately many of the organizations that we come across in the marketplace fail miserably at this mission. I have found that individuals with an attitude of servitude and humility typically succeed in providing great customer service. They follow the Golden Rule of treating others as they also would wish to be treated. They are typically individuals that are very bright and amiable. They are also great multi-takers and diligent in performing their obligations. Following are some tips for providing great customer service:

1. Make Eye Contact: Making visual contact with your client when you are speaking or listening will let them know that you are engaged. It also will transmit a message of sincerity and honesty.

2. Smile: Whether you are meeting with a client in person or over the phone it is necessary to smile. Smiling will help communicate enthusiasm and confidence. Your smile will generate acceptance for the customer.

3. Get back to your customers promptly: As technology progresses, the expectations from our clients increase as there is a greater sense of immediate gratification. Long gone are the pre-cell phone days where a customer would patiently wait for an answer. Manage your time efficiently and properly communicate the expectations. If you cannot get back to them promptly, find a way to let them know when you will get back to them and follow through with this promise.

4. Keep relationships alive by nurturing them: Understand what makes your clients "tick" and cater to their needs. Celebrate their accomplishments and constantly communicate with them even if they are not active. This will show that you care. People do not care how much ,you know unless they know how much you care.

5. Make people feel good: Always be a positive mood inducer, and avoid negative interactions. Service is given, hospitality is felt. Remove the word NO from your vocabulary.

6. Take notes: Carry a pencil, pen, tablet, smart phone at all times so that you can take notes. Do not depend on your memory.

7. Follow up and follow up more: Clients will appreciate your diligence in keeping their interest in mind. Anticipate problems rather than solving them.

8. Believe: Believe in yourself, your company, and its products and services.

CHAPTER TWO:

RETAIL VS. TRADE SALES

Within the U.S. tile and marble industry there are many companies that are dedicated to both retailing and wholesaling functions. This is true for many other organizations dedicated to interior home finishes as well as others in the apparel and electronic distribution business. It is difficult to take a blanket approach for all industries and all organizations; therefore, the following section is mainly dedicated to entities that have a retail component, as well as an outside trade customer component. There are many similarities to both of these areas and most of the smaller organizations will be forced to have the same people doing both functions. The salespeople dedicated to these functions will have similar traits previously highlighted in the Art of Selling chapter. Individuals focused on the retail component perhaps are not required to be as independent or aggressive in seeking out new business. Their focus is generally more towards attending the needs of a client which has already manifested an interest in their product by walking into a store. By the same token we cannot lose sight of the necessity for the sales force dedicated to this retail component to be professional and pro-active in the manner that they service their clients and perform their follow up. Retail sales personnel will likely require more patience in dealing with buyers that are indecisive or require more "hand-holding" with their selections and recommendations. The sales force dedicated to the outside trade customer base will require some autonomy and pro-activeness in seeking out a customer base that continuously uses the organization's products and services, but are probably sourcing these from a competing entity, if not currently sourcing from the organization. The trade transactions will sometimes have longer decision making periods which will require much follow-up and diligence on the part of the sales force. The trade transactions also will, on occasion, require the salesperson to "make the sales pitch" to a number of individuals or entities vs. just one or two in the retail process. Construction trade sales made via an architect in the U.S. usually require a selection by the architect, approval by the owner, support by the general contractor, and, ultimately, a purchase by the labor contractor. These are four different decision makers who have very different goals and interests that can either help or deter the sales proposition. Regardless of whether you are focused on retail or trade sales, it is important to remember that people buy from people that they like and those who show a keen interest in keeping the buyer's interest at heart.

RETAIL SALES

For retail oriented organizations the "store" becomes the business. The location of the store is key to traffic generation. The store design and layout also are very important to make the selection process easy for the consumer. In addition to the design there are other practical components to create a successful retail environment. Creating a uniformity of sales processes, as well as visual and olfactory stimulus, is pro-actively managed by the most sophisticated retailers.

In addition to the store, there is also a sales technique that is known as the retail sales model which helps us understand the business component of the sales? It is an objective model that can be tracked and managed:

> **Retail Sales Model =**
> **Market > Store Traffic > Selection > Close Ratio >**
> **Average Order = Average GP$**

In order to increase sales you must increase in any one of the following areas:

1. **Increase Market** = This part of the model is probably the most challenging of the components. This requires ma comprehensive

marketing campaign that is designed to create demand for your products and services over and beyond what currently exists. If an organization is dedicated to selling automobiles it has a market of individuals who are in the need of purchasing a vehicle or renewing their lease. Marketing would help these individuals identify your organization as one of the potential resources for their needs. Marketing would also help try to convince other drivers not currently needing a new vehicle to upgrade or add to their current collection by tapping into their capricious desire to purchase something that they do not need. This component of the retail sales model is very difficult and expensive to manage. It is the responsibility of the organization to do so at a macro level. The sales representatives have a very small impact on this component. The most they can do is market the organization by word of mouth, emailing, cold calling, etc. These initiatives can minimally impact the overall market but will definitely impact an increase in traffic.

2. **Increase Traffic** = Via advertising the organization will create traffic into the stores. There also are cases where there is an absence of advertising due to the amount of time the organization has been in business in a particular location. This brand recognition is what helps drive consumers that need your product or service to your doors. This component is also dominated by the organization at a macro level. The sales representative can participate in helping this process. They are able to focus their efforts on repetitive product consumers considering, if and when successful, they will essentially create a loyal core customer for their future revenue generation. The retail sales associate also directly impacts the possibility of referral generation. A large percentage of retail traffic will come from referrals. A happy customer will usually tell a couple of friends about their experience. (Unhappy customers will tell three times as many people about their bad experience). The retail sales associates should ensure that their time with the customer will generate the desire to share their service with others. The aggressive sales associates will find ways to ask their clients for referrals by manifesting the verbal interest or leaving the customer with referral cards that can be distributed to friends and family.

3. **Increase Selections** = It is assumed that a certain percentage of the traffic visiting the retail stores will make selections. Depending on the type of product, the selection and purchase process has a different time cycle. Some products are selected and purchased on the spot. Others have a longer selection and decision making process due to the nature of the expense or permanence of the purchase. The sales and customer service personnel are fundamental to increasing selections. To this end it is important for the organization to define a customer retail experience that meets the consumer's needs.

4. **Increase Close** Ratio of converted selections to orders by follow-up, service and competitive pricing. The sales representative is responsible for following the process and building relationship with the potential consumers. The follow-up provided by the sales representative will ensure that the customer is served to their fullest potential. This process also will help provide healthy organizational feedback for the "lost" transactions. Many times these transactions could have been closed with deeper inventories, cheaper pricing, or broader selections. The organization may or may not choose to remedy these type situations depending on the importance and resources. At the very least, the organization should never lose transactions due to a lack of service on the part of the sales representative or any other member of the organization.

5. **Increase Average** order by up-selling complimentary products or maintaining high prices. Maximizing average pricing is a focus of most organizations. Those who are successful are capable of achieving premium returns on their investments. It is important for the organization to clearly understand the niche of the market which it is serving. The sales representative needs to understand and communicate this value added incentive to the potential clients during the purchasing process. Product knowledge, confidence, and reliability are crucial to this component. Many organizations also will offer complimentary products that are available to the consumer's primary transaction. A swimsuit retaile could complement the transaction with cover-ups and or sandals while a flooring retailer can also sell the cleaning and maintenance products. In order to

master this component the sales representative should be engaged in understanding the products being offered as well as the psyche of the consumer during the purchasing process. The organization should focus on providing the proper training and products so that the sales team can maximize their efficiency.

6. The Objective of each component within the retail sales model is to increase GP$. Focusing on each component individually will create a mathematical increase of GP$. When the sales representative is capable of increasing or maximizing all of the components at the same time, the organization's profitability will increase exponentially as long as expenses do not increase accordingly. Following is an example for XYZ Retail company:

XYZ Retail Model

XYZ's retail component is the most important part of the business due to cash, higher margins, and market demands of service and design. The salespeople should be tracking all of the above. The store leaders should meet with each individual weekly to ensure they are measuring and improving these indicators. The manager in conjunction with the sales professional should set budget benchmarks as targets. The manager should spend more time with those not meeting the targets.

An example for the Chicago store would be:

Weekly traffic = 50
Close-ratio (cr) = 50-70 prct (?)
Average order = $750
Average GP %= 40%
Average GP $= $300
Week traffic 50 x 50cr = 25 orders x $750 = $18,750 x
40%GP = $7,500GP$ per week

An example for a retail focused individual depending on the number of customers serviced would be:

Week traffic 10 x 50cr = 5 orders x $750 = $3,750

If the salesperson is achieving only $3,750 per week with retail they can achieve $15,000 per month with retail and try to complement with an additional $5,000 per week with trade sales which would yield

$20,000 per month for a total sales budget of $35,000 per month = $420,000 per year.

Retail Sales Budgets

The annual sales budgets can be broken down to daily objectives that should be measured and monitored by the sales representative daily. Furthermore the sales representative should also generate a "pipeline" budget of activity required of them to reach the invoicing target. These "pipeline" indicators could include:

1. Customer quotes and selections (should be twice the sales budget if close ratio is 50%)
2. Order entry
3. Order shipping and invoicing

Monitoring tools for managers at XYZ Company:

DAILY

> Review traffic kept by reception and sales - salesmanager daily. Review hand written quotes and customer selections-sales manager daily.
> Review ABC Software order entry - sales manager.
> Review invoicing report by ABC Software-sales manager daily, general manager weekly, controller daily for pricing corrections, etc.

WEEKLY

> During sales meeting discuss weekly achievements and opportunities - general manager.

MONTHLY

> Review sales person achievements, products sold, customers purchased - sales manager, general manager, and controller.

Discuss the results with the individual team members on a one-on-one basis by general manager together with sales manager at least monthly; and more often with new sales representatives or those that are struggling. Keep in mind that recognizing our weaknesses is usually contrary to our human nature. Oftentimes, you will have great sales representatives that do not know how to utilize their skill set. It is up to the manager to recognize this weakness and help complement by providing direction and training if and when time permits.

TRADE SALES

Some organizations will conduct both retail and trade sales. At times the sales representatives will be required to focus on both components in order to achieve success. Other organizations might have two different sales teams focusing on each segment. There are different characteristics required of each segment, although most successful sales representatives are capable of performing both. The mathematical trade sales model is inspired by the retail model and by the notion that trade sales is a numbers game. The more you are exposed to your customer the more you sell.

Trade sales model:

Market > visits > selections > quotes > orders > average order = Average GP$

1. **Market**= Within the company's geographical area exists a potential customer base of entities that use the organization's product or service. This market will often depend on macro-economic influences and will expand and contract depending on the specific environment. From the 1990's to 2008 there was a very buoyant construction and real estate market in South Florida. Due to the financial crisis of 2008, this market became very dormant up until 2013. The amount of trade customers during the crisis was 1/3 what it had been during the previous decade. The focus during downturn periods such as these is more geared toward quality than quantity. It is important for the sales leaders to understand their market capacity and therefore allocate the necessary resources for the desired objectives. No matter how talented your sales force is it is difficult to make a living selling swimsuits in Alaska.

2. **Customer visits**= I cannot stress enough the fact that sales representatives dedicated to outside trade customers need to be on the road visiting customers. This is the one component of the trade sales model that the organization and sales representative can most easily impact. The more visits and customer exposure you have, the more you will sell. GUARANTEED! This component is so important

that I will dedicate the entire next chapter to discussing customer visits and share some techniques to help individuals perform the visits with higher rates of success.

3. **Customer selections**= I know of very few companies that can dedicate their sales force to just visiting customers. For most organizations the visits need to have a purpose. I will elaborate more on the visit objectives in the following chapter, but for most organizations the basic objective of a visit is to make a sale. In most cases a precursor to a sale has to be the buyer's selection of your product. In these cases it is not sufficient for the sales associate to merely visit a client. The sales associate needs to ensure that the visits bear fruit via product selections. Often times this process is enhanced by "listening". The client will let us know what he/she needs if we ask the right questions. Once we have defined the need or want, all we have to do is show up and deliver. This process requires much diligence and follow- up in order to increase success. Customer Relationship Manager software (CRM) can be very helpful in tracking both visits and selections. Make sure you create your own CRM.

During the late 90's I was managing an outside sales force of 6 individuals with a $9,000,000 revenue budget. There were two particular individuals who would consistently sell $1,500,000 per year, which was a great achievement. There was, however, a very big difference in how this was achieved. The more successful of the two individuals reached this objective with only six customers. The second individual did so with over one hundred customers. The second individual would spend his time on the road visiting over one hundred customers per month who purchased on average $1,000 per month. The first individual would spend two-three hours per day visiting with each customer on a weekly basis and would sell $20,000 to $30,000 per month to each one of them. The second individual was more focused on quantity than on quality. He would make over 10 times more visits than the first individual but was generating the same amount of revenue. By the same token he created the burden for the organization to serve one hundred clients vs. six. My point is that quantity is not always key. Quantity and quality go hand-in-hand and visits need to generate selections.

4. **Quotes**= Once a buyer selects a product, they will typically want a quote. In many cases the selection and quote will go hand in hand. On occasions there will be one entity that makes a selection and another entity that receives the quote. This happens often with developers and/or designers who are most concerned about the aesthetics of the building, while the general contractor and/or owner are very concerned about the budget of the building, and will have a purchasing entity that is designed to purchase the selected product at the best value. It is crucial for the sales representatives to track quote values. This will help them measure customer success rates, and, at the same time, allow them to track their pipeline of business potential.

5. **Orders**= The visits, selections, and quotes are a waste of time if ultimately an order is not placed and shipped to the customer. Successful sales people are constantly measuring their quote to order conversion ratio and following up with their clients. Many times clients will compare your quotes and products with the competition to ensure that they are purchasing the best product at the best value. It is during this process that the sales representative needs to be closest to the buyer so that they can identify any of the modified requirements or pricing propositions that need to be made in order to achieve the order. Successful sales representatives will ask for the order, realizing that it is hard to say "no" for human beings that like each other. Think about it...you have $100 available to purchase a nice pair of shoes that you need. You have identified two different pairs at two different stores which are both satisfactory to your needs. Both of the stores had lovely and service-oriented sales representatives that helped you try on the shoes and spent time informing you of the benefits and care requirements. You are more likely to purchase the pair of shoes from the sales representative that asks you for the order vs. the one that merely helps you and allows you to go about your day. Human beings have a sense of engagement and commitment

towards people that meet their needs, and it is difficult to reject their requests.

6. **Average order & average GP\$**= This component of the trade sales model is identical to the retail sales model. Increasing average orders and average GP\$ on a consistent basis will help generate more total GP\$ on an annual basis. The numbers don't lie! Often times a 1% difference to the bottom line will separate success from failure. Many companies do not share profit with their sales force, therefore, the focus is more on the average order value and unit pricing vs. profitability. Regardless, the result will be the same and it is important for the sales leader or company leader to realize the impact that pro-actively managing this process may have. Following is an example on how to implement the Outside Trade Customer Sales Model within XYZ company.

XYZ Outside Trade Customer Sales Team:

There are salespeople that are more suitable for outside sales as they generally are more confident in their ability to hit the road and generate new opportunities. These individuals should be required to spend at least 80% of their week on the road = 32 hours = 20 customer visits. These should be measured daily if possible. The 8 hours inside should be spent helping support retail needs or following up on previous quotes or orders. These people will require some inside customer service logistical support.

Other sales people will be 50/50 in and out to meet retail needs, as well as increase outside exposure. Others will be in 80% and out 20%.

Sales Person 1: (Market) > (Customer visits = 20) > (Customer selections = 10) > (Quotes = 9) > (Orders=6) > (Average order = $5,000) > (Average GP$ = $2,000) = Total GP$ $12,000

Sales Person 2: (Market) > (Customer visits = 14) > (Customer selections = 7) > (Quotes = 6) > (Orders=4) > (Average order = $5,000) > (Average GP$ = $2,000) = Total GP$ 8,000

Sales Person 3: (Market) > (Customer visits = 6) > (Customer selections = 3) > (Quotes = 2) > (Orders=1) > (Average order = $5,000) > (Average GP$ = $2,000) = Total GP$ 2,000

CREATING AN OUTSIDE SALES TRADE CUSTOMER PLAN:

It is likely that the outside opportunities are higher in value but more difficult to close successfully due to competition. Relationship building is crucial as the target buyer represents continuous revenue dollars over a longer period of time. Within this area time management is crucial as it generally takes the same amount of time to develop a $1,000,000 year customer as it does to develop a $200,000 per year customer. Following a detailed sales plan will help this process. Many people do not follow or believe in sales plans but I think of it as follows:

> If you launch a sailboat from Miami in a southeastern direction without an engine or route it is possible you will end up reaching a beautiful island with beautiful people and have a great time. It is also possible you will get lost in the Bermuda Triangle and never be heard from again!
>
> Vs.
>
> Launching a sailboat from Miami using charts, wind, and engines to reach a pre-planned desired location, you know for sure you'll encounter a beautiful place with fun people.
>
> Many sales representatives are successful despite not having the need to plan. They are lucky!

They have a great product, are in a great market, or possess great talent that overcomes their lack of planning. In most cases, I find that these components do not create consistent success. Those sales representatives found with the same products, in the same markets, with great talents, who plan well, will generally be more successful for longer periods of time. Sales plans are not always successful, but at least they provide a compass and plan of action that will increase the chances of success.

In 1999, I was managing an outsides sales force with a $9,000,000 annual revenue budget. South Florida was in the midst of a construction bonanza. Our company was fortunate to have a great reputation and team of individuals focusing on the market trends. We had invested the time and money to create a program dedicated to the medium to larger size track home builders working on developments of 100 to 500 houses per year. One of the sales individuals that I recruited to help promote this program (I will call him Billy) was a natural salesperson for this market. He was a Cuban-American that had grown up in a family dedicated to the flooring business. He was a dynamic and extroverted "go-getter" who was quick to connect with the mostly Latin contractor base in Miami. For two consecutive years, he was able to generate over $2,000,000 in revenues annually with no more than 3 clients per year. He was in a zone. Unfortunately Billy was not very disciplined or diligent in his follow-up and/or planning. He became comfortable. By 2003, Billy was struggling to sell $600,000 per year. The construction bonanza was starting to slow down and more competitors were entering the market. Billy was losing part of his core customer base due to lack of service. Everyone still liked him and would see him socially, but they would not do business with him. He was not able to recover and by 2005 was replaced by a young dynamic individual who was capable of connecting with people and following diligent strategic plans. Don't become a Billy!

The first step to creating a sales plan should be to establish an objective. There are two types of targets:

1. Needs based objectives
2. Expectation based objectives

Personally I try to combine both when establishing targets with my sales team. I recommend you do the same. The needs based objectives are dependent on the company or sales associate's needs.

Needs Based Example a: The company needs to generate $400,000 in EBIDTA; therefore, needs two sales representatives selling $1,000,000 each at a 40% margin = $2,000,000 revenues = $800,000 in GP$. Assuming $400,000 in expenses the company will reach the objective.

Needs Based Example b: The sales representative needs to make $80,000 per year and receives an 8% gross revenue commission. The sales representative needs to sell $1,000,000 per year.

The expectation based objective is more market driven and will take into consideration opportunity costs. The manager needs to consider the cost of having an individual taking up market space and management time. This organizational cost has to be considered when evaluating the profitability of a sales representative. When setting annual objectives it is important to make sure that they are profitable.

The second step to setting a sales plan is establishing how the sales representative intends to reach their objectives by identifying the intended customers as well as products to be used.

1. The Core Customer Revenue
2. The Target Customer Revenue
   – Developed from a Prospect Customer List

The objective for all sales representatives should be to have enough core customers to reach their annual objectives continuously. How do we define a core customer? For each organization and each sales representative the definition will vary, but, overall, it will be clients that are committed and are continuously purchasing products from your organization. It is highly unlikely (although it does happen on occasion) that a customer will purchase 100% of their products from you. Many clients purposefully avoid "putting all their eggs in one basket" and will seek out a variety of vendors. During most of my career I defined core customers as those purchasing at least 50% of their needs from my company with a minimum of XXXXXX $ per year. During the boom years the minimum was $200,000 per year. After the crisis, I would consider clients core when they would give us 50% of their business and a minimum of $50,000 per year. Setting a minimum puts thing into perspective for the sales representatives as they focus on managing their time. Remember that it usually takes the same amount of time to develop a $50,000 core customer as it does a $200,000 core customer. Once they are developed, the time spent with each should be different as the amount of purchases create more operational activity, but, if we assume the sales associate is mainly dedicated to the development process (as they should be) the time spent will be very similar. Sales professionals should always have the objective to become their core customer's number one supplier. If you are not number one, become number two because eventually number one will slip up and create an opportunity for you to grow from number two to number one.

New core customers are continuously being developed. Prior to becoming a core customer they should be considered a target customer. The target customer is one with whom the sales associates spend a bulk of their efforts. They are customers that have the potential of purchasing 50% of their business from your organization with a minimum of XXXXXX $ per year. They are those who are either new to the market or are likely purchasing from your competition. Prior to becoming a core customer they should be considered a prospect. I highly recommend that all sales representatives keep an active list of prospect clients. I have always described the difference between target and prospect customers as follows: Most of us, regardless of our lifestyles, have felt attraction toward other individuals. We are attracted to them for many reasons: external beauty, eyes, physique, personality, intellect, humor, etc. People to whom we are attracted are equivalent to our prospects. Just because we are attracted to them doesn't mean we necessarily want to date them or spend time with them. We typically have higher standards of criteria that they should meet to reach this level. Just because we date them and spend time with them, it does not mean we want to spend the rest of our life with them. Prospects are customers that we find attractive. We need to research and identify whether they meet our higher standards of criteria prior to establishing them as a target. Once we have them as a target and are courting them, we will mutually decide whether to marry and make them a core. It is good to have a lot of prospects, as you never do know how dating will go.

Viewing your customers as relationships is more than just a fun way of approaching this strategy. Customers require us to nurture them just as our personal relationships do. Eventually many of our customers will become some of our greatest personal relationships. Many of us have heard about CRM software. These Customer Relationship Managers are designed to help us more efficiently manage the relationships that we create. The greater the number of relationships, the more help we need. Can you imagine having to keep up with 100 different girlfriend or boyfriend birthdays? Celebrating someone's birthday is only one of the components of the nurturing process. Can you think of other ways that we can cater to someone's ego? The more you know about a person the better you will become at creating a significant relationship that can withstand time, trials, and tribulations. Remember that being genuine is one of the most important aspects of relationship and client building. Knowing details about your client or significant other doesn't mean that you have to agree with or become like your target. Here are some of the details I find that you should try to know about your customers:

1. Birthday	5. Anniversary	9. Religion
2. Family Names	6. Favorite Food	10. Travel Interest
3. Sports Teams	7. Favorite Drink	11. Car Types
4. Hobbies / Interest	8. Politics	12. Shirt Size

One of the keys to the nurturing process is to gather this information without the customer necessarily knowing that you are gathering it. (Not because gathering the information is wrong, but because you do not want to submit your clients to a questionnaire.) This information can be very helpful if used correctly at the right moment. Most of us enjoy receiving gifts as well as having our ego stroked. Can you imagine being able to give your top customer a cruise for him and his wife Jane to their favorite destination for their 20th anniversary? How about avoiding the discussion of touchy current events or sports results, which might create some sense of animosity? No matter what, being diligent in the manner that you develop your customer base is very important. If you are not paying attention, it is likely that someone else is!

Once we have a good list of Prospect, Target, and Core customers it is now time to create a list of activities for each and every one of them. The activities are for the sales representative to follow and should have an established objective as well as deadline so that these are achieved in a timely manner. These activities should be followed and reviewed weekly so that they can be modified and enhanced as the relationships become more active. The monitoring process should also help you determine the clients with whom you have invested a lot of time and effort with very little to show for it. Upon occasion, we are better off abandoning customers if their conduct or lack thereof is detrimental to our success. This is very difficult for a sales representative to do.

There are only two examples of times when I have been involved in abandoning a customer. The first example was carried out by an Outside Sales Representative that had been with our organization for twenty years. He had been in the industry for thirty years and was very well known. He had developed a "relationship" with almost every single potential client within his geographical territory. He had a keen sense of customer service and followed his clients via a methodical "vending route" type strategy. There was one particular client that was very savvy and took advantage of the sales representative's good nature. Over a period of two years the client would have the sales representative bring him samples and provide quotes constantly. Unfortunately the customer would never buy anything. Eventually we learned that the client was using our samples and quotes to achieve better pricing from our competition. Needless to say we decided to cut our losses and find better ways to invest our time. This was not easy but it paid off in the long-run. We did this without directly telling the customer, as it is not recommendable to burn any bridges. We essentially began to raise our pricing and not have the required samples available when the client would call. We never did business with the client again, as they no longer used us as a resource, and after a couple of years closed their business for personal reasons.

The second example was with a customer that I personally handled due to the demanding nature of the client. The client was an ego-driven, abusive individual who looked to squeeze his suppliers to death by constantly negotiating pricing, paying late, and finding ways to purchase the same products elsewhere. For three years we catered to this client's needs and invested countless service hours, and eventually, the client sent us a large purchase order for a substantial size project requiring a very expensive, German special order product. Three months after having received and stocked the product for the client, he called to cancel the order. He had found an alternate product cheaper. This created a huge financial burden on our organization. We could have chosen the legal path by litigating the issue and demanding payment. Instead we decided to close the client's account. For an entire year we did not hear from the client or have any interaction. Eventually, I started receiving invitations from the client for golf tournaments and social networking events. Within two years we had once again established a personal relationship and he began using our products on our terms. We eventually became great personal friends, with the understanding that we could only do business on terms that mutually benefited each other. I am convinced that the client respected us more for not bending to his abusive behavior.

My point with these examples is that there will be occasions those certain clients are not good for us as professionals or for our organization. This is OK. We do not have to be all things to all people. We have to find a way to create value for those whom in turn appreciate the service and product we provide. There are many of these type clients in the market.

In addition to the daily activity list previously mentioned, we should also create a product list that identifies the particular products and services being utilized by each client. This list will help us keep track of the products that we have identified as matches for our client's needs. This way we can ensure that these products are well sampled and supported. We can also easily identify replacements when products are discontinued. This list will also help us forecast the possible product consumption which will help our management and logistics team ensure that we have enough to satisfy customer demands. Once this plan is complete, we should end up with a structure that looks like this:

The core and target customers form the base upon which you will build your daily activities and promote products to generate the desired gross profit dollars.

CHAPTER THREE:
TRADE CUSTOMER VISITS

Performing customer visits is one of the most rewarding activities that a sales representative dedicated to a trade customer base can perform. Not only are the visits economically rewarding but they can also be very motivating for people that enjoy personal contact and communication. For some individuals the visits can also be very intimidating. The truth is, a large percentage of sales representatives have a small portion of bashfulness that creates the need for exertion on their part to overcome this obstacle. By the same token, there are many customer types that are not very kind when it comes to hosting visitors. These clients can be rude at times and this creates further aversions for the sales representatives. The customer's personality plays a key component within the visiting process. The depth of the relationship with the customer can also be very influential. Regardless of the customer's personality and/or the relationship, visits should always be conducted in a professional manner.

A customer visit should essentially be nothing less than visiting a relative for whom you have much respect. You should feel comfortable and natural enough to be yourself and amiable without becoming too familiar. The more comfortable you are, the more likely the customer will be comfortable as well. Earlier I discussed a tool used for filtering employees called the Predictive Index. This tool can also be very useful in identifying your client's personality type. There is a different strategic proposition that should be made for each personality type. Analytical customers will be very interested in the technical aspects of the products or services while creative customers will probably be more interested in the aesthetical values of your presentation. Regardless of the customer type, there should always be an objective to your visit. I have identified two different types of visits with a third component that should always be an objective (the ultimate objective is generating revenue which in turn generates gross profit dollars):

1. Pro-active product/service promotion not requested by the customer. Whenever we identify a product or service that is suitable for a potential client, we must make that product or service known to the client. If we do not make the product or service known, it is unlikely anyone else will. It is our duty to schedule product promotion and presentation times for the clients we feel the products are suitable.

2. Re-active product / service promotion requested by the customer. Many times a client will call us to request a product that they know we carry. These calls are very pleasant as the client is pro-actively opening the opportunity for us to solicit their business. It is crucial to rapidly respond to 100% of these requests even if we do not think we can completely satisfy the customer's needs. At the very least, they will appreciate the service and hopefully continue to call us for other similar requests.

3. Gathering information from the client / Asking questions. I have dedicated an entire chapter to the importance of listening. Gathering information from a client is a form of listening. Successful salespeople will gather information during every single customer encounter.

All customer visits require preparation. The sales representative should have a positive state of mind and be capable to transmit confidence and excitement to the buyer. Listening to inspiring music prior to the visit can help set a positive state of mind. Envisioning a positive outcome of the visit also will help. Having knowledge of the customer's needs and/or objectives is helpful so that the value proposition is customized to their needs. It is important for the sales professional to feel comfortable making a presentation. I highly recommend that all sales professionals receive at least some basic training regarding speaking in public.

This will go a long way in helping create confidence when speaking to others. Having a prepared presentation also will help although it can also be dangerous to "show up and throw up". Essentially this happens when a sales representative is overly focused on communicating the product's values without properly identifying whether the client deems that the values are important for them. Keep in mind the expensive remote control example. No matter how expensive a remote control and the amount of applications it can manage, it is not important if the client only wants to change channels and manage the volume on the TV. Highlighting the values and features for the client will be annoying and eventually a waste of time.

Remember that highly successful sales professionals ask many questions. These questions need to be integrated into the presentation so that it does not become a monologue given by the sales professional. It is much better to have the potential client engage in the presentation. This will help them retain the information and possibly generate excitement that monologues do not achieve. Once the visit is finished, it is important for the sales representative to document the results of the visit and whether follow-up action items are required.

PRO-ACTIVE PRODUCT / SERVICE PROMOTION

These visits can be scheduled or non-scheduled (cold). The scheduled visits are perhaps easier to conduct as the chances of rejection are limited. Scheduled Promotional visits are designed to make the customer aware of a product or service that you carry. This is a product or service that has already been identified as a possible need for the client. When possible, it is best that the product or service that is being presented have a "market value" that has been previously identified by the organization. At the very least this "market value" can be communicated to the client for their personal benefit and market edification even when they might not have a particular need for a product. Within the ceramic tile industry we would rely a lot on technology to create this new "market value". We were able to highlight the technological advancements of the newer products which, at the very least, created interest for the buyer regardless of whether they could utilize the product based on the particular aesthetic or technical values. An example of this is when the ceramic factories started making "slim" tile. The new slim tile was 3-4mm thick vs. the traditional 10-12mm thick products. The new thickness was designed for certain re-model markets and was able to reduce transport cost by 60% due to the lighter weights. Almost all of the architectural and designer customers would find this new technology interesting even if they did not have an immediate practical use for it at the time. Another technique used when making new product or service presentations is having something to create a "WOW" factor. They are typically products or services that are not very practical or high in demand but are very appealing conceptually. These "WOW" products are used to create interest and excitement while at the same time presenting more mundane items that will probably be purchased more readily. No matter the type of product, it is important that the sales representative be prepared to leave the potential buyer with samples and literature for further analysis. I do not always recommend that the samples or literature be left on the spot. Being able to return the following day or a couple hours later creates another customer visit and further interaction that can be valuable. The circumstances should dictate whether it is best to leave the samples on the spot or to return. Regardless, the samples and literature should be available immediately. Having to wait for something that you want for too long a period can create a sense of lack of professionalism and "kill" the spur of the moment enthusiasm.

REACTIVE PRODUCT / SERVICE PROMOTION

These customer visits are very rewarding as the potential for rejection is very minimal.

One of the objectives that we have with our customers is that they will think of us, our company, and our product when they have a need. When they call or email us requesting to see something for a specific need we have achieved this objective. It is important during these visits to make sure that we have properly filtered the request by understanding the need. Asking questions is once again fundamental to this process. When the product is needed, the quantity of the product needed, the intended use of the product, and the desired price of the product are all very important questions for these type presentations. Can you think of others for your industry?

INFORMATION GATHERING

All visits should have a component of information gathering. We have already discussed the information gathering required for the customer file and nurturing process. There is also certain information that needs to be gathered pertaining to the specific visit as discussed in the previous section. What other type of information should we gather from our customers? The more we gather the better prepared we will be to make value propositions that help build the relationship and create continuity. How about the following:

How much of my product does the customer consume per year?
How many decision makers does the customer have?
What are the Value Incentive Services Added (VISA) that are important to them?
Who is my competition?
What does my competitor do that is perceived as VISA by the customer?
Who does my customer work for and what is important to their customer?
What are the current projects/needs of the client that I am not servicing?
What can I do to increase the current business wit the customer?
What can I do to attain 100% of the customer's business?

VISITS FOLLOW UPS

We obtain the results that we inspect, not what we expect. The amount of sales professionals who do not properly follow-up their activities is unbelievable. Creating lists of action items to be accomplished with each client will help prevent a lack of attention. The management team should also be involved in reviewing and discussing activities with the sales team as often as necessary. The review process should be dynamic enough to be able to modify action items and strategy based on the activities that are generating results. Avoid going through the motions without results. Most of us that work in sales are in the business of generating revenue, not promoting product.

CHAPTER FOUR:
SALES CONCLUSION

Selling can be one of the most rewarding jobs for those who enjoy it. Many people possess natural talents which helps them sell successfully. It is, however, important to recognize that putting in some effort in preparing the mind, body, and spirit beyond the natural talent will help elevate the results, as well as the profession. Having confidence is equally important as being humble enough to listen and obey (follow instructions). If/when we ask the right questions, the clients will always tell us what they want. All we have to do is deliver!

PART III:
OPERATIONS & ADMINISTRATION

The Operations and Administrative departments of companies are just as important as the sales organizations, and, therefore should be managed much the same. Very often, I see ownership groups and management teams that view these divisions as secondary priorities manifested by the time and dedication given to insuring smooth and efficient integration. It is true that these departments would not be needed if revenues are not being generated. By the same token, it is also very true that revenue generation will suffer if there is not good operational and administrative team members in place to offer the service and continuity required. The leadership and communication tips provided in previous chapters can and should be applied to the Operations and Administrative departments. Excellent individuals provide excellent results; and, personnel development and training should be a fundamental part of the manager's objectives. Operations and Administration are very general terms and can define many different types of duties within companies. I generally refer to Operations as the logistical, warehousing, and purchasing components, while Administration includes the financial, accounting, and human resources components.

As with sales, there are certain characteristics that describe people whom managers typically recruit for these departments. Remember, there are always exceptions to the rule and it is always very dangerous to generalize. For the most part, individuals working in the Operations and Administration departments will be:

*Detail-oriented Analytical Responsible Reliable Diligent Introverted
Team-oriented Assertive Honest Modest Confident Timely*

The nature of the personalities of these individuals is often times contrary to those of the salespeople. For this reason many organizations have a hard time getting sales, operations, and administration on the same page. Doing so requires diligence on the part of the management team, but is well worth the effort, as nothing will stop a well-oiled team that is firing all pistons in conjunction with one another.

Once again, humility and positive attitudes on the part of the team members are required to achieve a harmonious environment. A mentality of servitude towards the sales associates and their customer objectives will help play up to the typically egocentric sale types. For some of the team members this will be a hard attitude to implement on an ongoing basis. Constant communication and team building on the part of the management team will help everyone involved.

Following are quick summaries of what I consider important for the total integration of the Operational and Administrative departments. Future chapters will discuss specific illustrations and approaches on carrying out the departmental functions.

Purchasing & Merchandising - The leader should be an intelligent, dynamic, multi-tasking individual who possesses a solid work ethic. His/Her motivation should be achieved internally by knowing that the job they are performing is very important. They should seek satisfaction through serving others but have sufficient backbone to defend the guidelines that accomplish efficient workflows. Those in the entire department should view their positions beyond operational 9-5 jobs by becoming engaged with the activities and results of the sales staff. They should be willing to dedicate time to continued education as well as vendor relationship development. They should be willing to become technical experts regarding the products for which they are responsible in the event they are needed as a resource to help a sales associate help a customer.

Warehousing & Logistics - The leader should be a meticulous and detailed leader who is capable of organizing and supervising the work of others. He/She should be customer-oriented and understand the customer life cycle. The department should strive to become a competitive advantage for the organization by doing the common things uncommonly well, such as storing and shipping products. The staff should be motivated and compensated according to their efforts. This department is typically ignored and taken for granted by many individuals within organizations, and, therefore, small acknowledgements go a long way in creating a sense of greater engagement.

Accounting – The leader should be an intelligent and ethical individual capable of understanding the overall macro-objective. He/She also should be capable of relationship building with fellow managers and/or clients, if necessary. The department should view their functions beyond recording debits and credits with a notion of how they can help impact the service that the company provides its clients and sales associates. Many times, the accounts receivable department and personnel can work directly against the interest of the sales efforts if there is not a constant stream of communication and common understanding. The accounts payable department has a similar impact on the purchasing efforts and should be communicating closely with the purchasing team and/or vendors when necessary. The staff closest to customer functions should be amiable and humble. By the same token, all team members should hold very high standards of efficiency, as well as help educate other company members about the improvements that can be made daily. Accounting typically records the numbers that result from other department's efforts. Seeking improvements and/or explanations of these numbers will help the entire organization. This department should avoid the "it's not my job" syndrome.

Human Resources- The leader should be a pro-active and dynamic goal-setter that understands the fact that the employees are the most valuable resources to the organization. He/She needs to know exactly how their job impacts the bottom line and constantly seek methods to improve recruiting of new individuals and training the existing individuals. Great communication is key within this department due to the fact that perceptions become realities, and employees will not always understand what you intend for them to understand. A de-motivated employee can be a cancer to the organization. The Human Resources team can help keep people motivated and engaged.

I recommend that all Operations and Administration team members learn and understand the fundamentals of the nature of the business--not just their jobs. Very often team members that work in these departments can get caught up on the "administration" functions and lose sight of the objectives of the organization. Quite frankly, a bookkeeper is not typically required to have an in-depth knowledge of product pricing or technical aspects. They can successfully help the organization keep appropriate books without specific knowledge regarding the business. It is, however, important that a bookkeeper understand the macro concepts of how the product purchased is made and taken to market. This knowledge will allow the bookkeeper to contribute more than just booking debits and credits. It will help them engage in the business and possibly help impact the bottom line. It is important for the entire team to row at the same time and in the same direction.

Cross-training between departments can be very powerful in getting your team rowing in the same direction. Having team members from one department work and learn the functions of other departments elevates the knowledge of the entire team as well as helps create empathy toward one another. The different team members will experience new challenges and see situations from different perspectives to which they are accustomed. It is also usually a fun process, as many team members will inevitably become bored with what they are doing if they have been doing it for a long time. The objective is not to have the team members perfectly trained in all aspects of all jobs. The objective is to provide each individual just enough insight to each of the functions so that everyone can work more efficiently with one another.

CHAPTER ONE:
PURCHASING & MERCHANDISING

The Purchasing function is one of the most important aspects of an organization in that when done properly a competitive advantage, as well as increase the margin of profitability, are potential outcomes. It is, although, important to remember that purchasing goes hand-in-hand with selling, as there is no need to purchase anything if the sales do not accompany the purchasing volume.

In 1996 I had been with Iberia Tiles for two years. I was in the process of completing my Management Training Department rotations which had given me experience within the warehouse, the customer service counter, purchasing, and sales. I had recently finished my purchasing department rotation during which time I successfully helped the Purchasing Manager organize the special order division. I was in the midst of finishing my Outside Sales Training when I received a call from our CEO who wanted to meet with me ASAP. During the meeting he informed me that he had been forced to terminate our current Purchasing Manager due to unethical behavior, and he offered me the Purchasing Manager's job. I was at once shocked by this news as I had worked closely with the Purchasing Manager and did not foresee his termination. I was also elated at being offered my first management position. I accepted the job on the spot and after thirty minutes of discussing the description and expectations of the position, the CEO informed me that within two days I would be travelling on my own to my first trade show in Spain. He was not able to accompany me due to other urgent matters needing his attention at one of our branches in Denver. His instructions for the trip to Spain were very clear: "Go, watch, listen, and learn about the suppliers." He continued, "Take good notes on everything you see, but don't purchase anything." My introduction to Purchasing was fast and furious. Soon after the Spanish buying trip, I realized that being given the responsibility for the purchase of $3,000,000 worth of inventory was a great vote of confidence in me on the part of our CEO. I also became very popular amongst our industry suppliers as I became the decision maker for purchases that represented a great deal of revenue to actual and future suppliers. The actual suppliers wanted to diligently ensure that their spot within our supplier mix was protected while new suppliers wanted to take advantage of the personnel change to become one of our resources. The next year was one of much learning and dedication to the purchasing process which has continued until present day.

I view the purchasing function at two separate macro levels: the first is the product identification, sourcing, and merchandising function; the second is the mechanical replenishment and ordering function for stock or order fulfillment. Both aspects are crucial to the organizational success and are able to be managed objectively in order to increase efficiency.

SOURCING AND MERCHANDISING

For most distribution and retail entities the sourcing and merchandising should be managed with an "outside-in" approach vs. an "inside-out" approach. The "outside-in" method focuses on identifying market (outside) needs and sourcing those products demanded by the market. The "inside-out" approach is used for unique products for which there is not an evident market demand and the entity creates an inside push out to the market in creating a demand. The inside-out approach will require more time and effort in creating a demand for the product to be promoted.

It is necessary for the purchasing team to be much attuned to the market needs. This can be achieved by methodically scheduling customer visits and sales team exposure. The sales team is usually the department closest to the market and should be the gateway to the customers. It is although, necessary to filter perceived sales and customer needs, being that resources are limited, and it is impossible for most organizations to purchase and carry everything that the market perceives to need. Within this process it is important to remember the commonly accepted 80/20 rule which proposes that 80% of an entity's sales will be achieved with 20% of the entity's products. It is important to clearly identify the 20% of the products that are necessary, and compliment them with the 80% that will help enhance the product differentiation and 20% sales that are needed.

There are three tools I recommend that every organization use in order to help objectively manage and organize the product sourcing process:

Tool 1 - Product Chart

The Product Chart is essentially a list of products that the organization has identified necessary to carry out the business objectives. These products are the ones that have been identified by the customers and sales team as fundamental to the company's goals. They can be both inventory and special order items. Essentially, they are the items that the management team needs to ensure are available to the market via the organization. This list should be limited to the products the organization has identified as important to promote.

Tool 2 - Product Cost

The Product Cost is a list of products that should include the same items as the Product Chart. The main difference is that this list will include detailed costs, as well as possible pricing for the products that the organization will encounter and possibly need over time. This document will allow the purchasing team to compare different supplier costs of similar products as well as margin objectives. It is essentially an organized way to store all possible product costs over time so that the entity has a single source product cost.

Tool 3 - Customer Price List

The Customer Price List will list only the products that the company is currently offering at the pricing levels approved by management. This document is used to communicate to the sales force the products that are supported by the purchasing team.

Positive and frequent communication between Purchasing and Sales is crucial to an efficient

Organization. The Purchasing Department needs to be empathetic toward the customer and sales needs. The sales team should understand of the challenges faced by the purchasing team. Purchasing and sales should be an extension of each other vs. polarized departments. Each will have the same objective of increasing gross profit dollars for the organization. Information systems should be used by purchasing to communicate important information regarding products and arrivals. By the same token, sales can communicate to purchasing the demand and usage of particular products so that they can be properly planned and forecasted. This flow of information is key to a successful and efficient organization.

THE PURCHASING CYCLE

The purchasing department should be responsible for sourcing and negotiating with vendors once a product or service is identified as being important for the company. In some organizations the General Manager will lead the sales and purchasing functions, especially when it comes to sourcing. Other organizations will rely on professional Purchasing Managers or Merchandisers. Not all industries are the same when it comes to product supply. Some industries have great barriers of entry and therefore are dominated by the supply side. The vendors are limited and have a greater deal of authority when choosing their distribution chains. On the other hand, also there exist industries with an over-abundance of supply whereby the distribution channels have many sources to choose from. In high supply markets, the distributors have more choices and greater control over the terms and conditions at which they buy products. Vendor relations are important to manage pro-actively. In most cases vendors should be viewed as "partners" who can support the organization's goals. Some vendors will try to influence the organization's decisions by promoting directly to the company's sales team or customer base. These efforts can be beneficial if managed well. They can also be detrimental if clear rules of conduct are not established for the vendors and sales team. Some vendors will on occasion try to influence demand via economic incentives. These incentives should always be via the company and upon approval of the management team.

Selecting the appropriate vendor is not always easy. The previously mentioned Product Chart and Product Cost files are designed to help this process. They achieve this by objectively documenting the particular product needed as well as listing the possible suppliers. Once the possible suppliers have been reviewed it is up to the Purchasing leadership to decide whom to purchase from. It is very important to develop personal relationships with all vendors. These relationships help get through the difficult situations. Despite the need of relationship management, I also recommend that an objective process be implemented when dealing with vendors. This objective process will help create equality amongst the possible providers. It also will help document the business conditions that are established between a buyer and vendor. The first step to implementing the objective buying process is by creating a vendor agreement. The vendor agreement will essentially be a piece of paper that documents the arrangements the company has reached with a particular vendor.

A vendor agreement should include:

Vendor Legal & Contact Information: People buy from people, but organizations buy from organizations. It is important to understand that an agreement between a purchaser and seller is backed by the companies that they each represent. Having a legal notion of the appropriate parties is important because personnel can change over periods of time. Purchasers do not want their business conditions to be altered negatively by departing sales representatives. Therefore documenting the legal entity that is backing the supply agreement is very important.

Supply Term: Establishing the time limits or lack thereof is important especially if the products being sold are time sensitive and/or service a particular part of the industry that is exclusive and niche driven.

Payment Terms: This is a mutual understanding at how the purchasing entity intends to pay the supplying entity. Typical terms would be cash, cash upon delivery (COD), credit payment allowed upon 30 days (Net 30), or longer depending on the industry. Consignment payment terms can also be typical and advantageous for certain industries.

Expected Purchases: This is essentially a projection of expected consumption of the particular product or service. This component can be dangerous for organizations that do not want purchasing restrictions to influence the accessibility to the product. At the very least, it is designed to create common expectations between the purchaser and buyer so that there are zero misunderstandings in the future.

Delivery Times: For most organizations "time is of the essence," and there should be established timely service expectations and commitments that are documented. This will help determine the way to act if and when the expectations are not met.

Pricing and Rebate Expectations: In most cases these expectations will be supported by addendums and price lists that are provided by the supplying entity. Companies will often establish their own customer pricing practices based on the practices conducted by their suppliers. Having these prices documented with a time frame allows for strategic planning on a continual basis.

Areas of Exclusivity: Many times products and services are acquired with the notion that the areas of representation will be exclusive to the organization. The exclusivity becomes part of the positive perception of difference of the product or service and would not hold the same value if it were not exclusive. Documenting the areas of exclusivity keep both parties honest by ensuring that the exclusivities and representations are being made according to the original agreement.

Marketing and Merchandising Support: It is not uncommon for many suppliers to provide their clients with marketing and merchandising support which is used to drive demand for their products. Oftentimes these incentives are more aggressive when companies are launching new products. It is not uncommon for the suppliers to minimize or eliminate these incentives as the product life cycles begin to mature. This helps eliminate their cost and increases their profit. Documenting and negotiating supplier incentives at the time of purchase are very important, as typically these can be incorporated into the life of the product or service. Remember that the squeaky wheel always gets the grease and if you don't ask, many times it will not be given.

Promotional Expectations: Most of the above components of the vendor buying agreement are documented and in benefit of the buying entity. It is not a bad idea to also provide your supplier with a promotional commitment. This commitment will oftentimes allow you to negotiate better incentives, and, at the very least, will help provide a framework from which you will try to increase your revenues. Ultimately, it is best to under-promise and over-deliver; therefore, use these expectations sparingly and when the benefits of making them justify the additional level of commitment.

Negotiating purchases with vendors is a very personal process. Each individual is different and will have a unique negotiating style. Embracing and learning from team member individuality is one of the things that I have enjoyed the most in my career. At the same time, there are certain aspects of the negotiation process which are commonly good to keep in mind. I have divided these aspects into two different purchasing profiles. The first I call Soldier Purchasing and the second I call Nomad Purchasing.

Soldiers by profession are some of the most disciplined individuals that you will find. By the same token, so is the Soldier Purchasing style. This style is influenced by a determined effort of creating efficiency, and is generally a no-nonsense straight forward time saving process. This purchaser will know exactly what they need and will not waste much time beating around the bush during the search process. The meetings with vendors will be established with agendas, subjects, and time limits. Typically enough information will be shared with the vendor in order to allow the vendor to make a value proposition that will meet the buyer's expectations. The buyer will typically execute quickly once they find a solution to their need.

The Nomad Purchasing style is more relaxed. It is a flexible style that seeks competitive advantages via products and from vendors that are in need of making a deal. The negotiations are long and drawn out processes designed to maximize the seller's discounts. The buyer shares relatively little information with the potential seller and will work in the realm of ambiguity. Both of these styles have their places and can be used by the same buyer for different scenarios.

The following are the purchasing traits that are common to both:

1. **Know your market** – It is fundamental that the person responsible for executing purchases knows the market cost and selling price for specific products. This is the only way to know whether a product is being purchased at a discount or premium.

2. **Expect a lot** – Create high expectations for your vendors because your clients will create high expectations for you. The vendors should be able to meet your expectations in the same way you meet your client's expectations. The vendors become your "partners" in delivery of the value incentive service added (VISA).

3. **Be respectful** – Although it is good to follow the adage that "a customer is always right," it is best not to act like a customer. What I mean by this is that it is best to be respectful and professional with your vendors. You can and should hold vendors to high expectations.

4. **Manage your time** – Do not allow your vendors to take up your time or the time of your team members. Many vendor representatives have nothing better to do than to "hang out" with you and your sales representatives. This is the way they create camaraderie and gather information for their value propositions. The time they spend does not always serve your best interest and therefore you need to manage the process. Time is usually on your side, especially with those vendors to whom you are important.

5. **Be neutral** – I recommend that you generally not purchase products or services based on emotion. Keep the business viability in mind and not your own personal preferences. Try not to show too much emotion or satisfaction with a product or service. Showing satisfaction can work against your negotiation process. On the other hand, try not showing too much dissatisfaction or arrogance as it could possibly work against you if the vendor is offended.

Once the product is sourced, the merchandising function becomes the primary focus of the management team. During the merchandising process it is important to communicate to the sales team and customer base why the product was chosen and how the product will satisfy the customer needs. Communicating the technical aspects that make the products unique, as well as its design characteristics and pricing, are important. I suggest that each organization have a uniform and organized manner of creating product data sheets for this purpose. Within this process, management and the purchasing team should think of marketing the product to their sales team. In turn, the sales team will use the same process to market their product to their customer base. Following this process will enhance the product performance.

During the merchandising process, the entity must consider:

a. Target Market

b. Pricing Communication

c. Marketing

d. Display Systems

e. Sampling Systems

f. Replenishment Schedule

Once all of the merchandising considerations have been implemented, the purchasing team can schedule the product arrival and promotion.

It is possible to purchase and sell products without going through the above process. It is not unusual for smaller organizations to have an owner purchase a product at a trade show. Sometime after the purchase, the product shows up at the warehouse unbeknownst to anyone. The product is stored and may or may not be discovered by a curious salesperson who may or may not share it with his/her colleagues. Six months later the owner will wonder why the product purchased did not perform to expectations. The merchandising process will not ensure product success, but it will eliminate any doubt whether the product has been promoted properly for success.

STOCK REPLENISHMENT

The stock replenishment and ordering functions are mechanical and logistical functions which are more operationally oriented. Attention to detail, persistence, and follow-up will help increase efficiency. A robust information system also will help the re-ordering process. At the very least, good inventory software should allow for the team to view available and incoming stock, track costing, and customer orders. The software should be able to report consumption in weekly or monthly increments. It should also be able to clearly identify back orders that need to be fulfilled. The purchasing team should review stock availability on a regular basis. Management should establish the reordering parameters. There are many different inventory and purchasing methods. I will not bore you with all of the details of each, but most of them are determinant on the financial capabilities or capital investment philosophy held by the ownership. The just-in-time inventory philosophy is perhaps the most aggressive method requiring lower capital investment with orders being fulfilled just in time, as the name suggests. This method will yield higher inventory turns at the risk of not having enough stock when the client has an immediate need. When abundant capital is available and the return being generated by the organization is desirable, a less aggressive approach can be used by holding high levels of stock in advance of the customer demands. This approach is speculative in nature and carries some calculated risks as it is possible for demands to drop and therefore create a higher level of inventory obsolescence and need for liquidation at lower or negative margins. By the same token, this method can help increase efficiencies with cost reduction for volume purchases as well as personnel reduction being that the inventory is purchased less often than using the just-in-time method. With all things being equal, it is probably best to find a balance between high inventory levels for commodity products and more of a just-in-time process for specialty products.

Regardless of the stock keeping unit philosophy, it is up to purchasing to make sure the sales team is clear regarding the company commitments toward customers. Most entities will require inventory review at least on a weekly basis. Sophisticated and experienced purchasers should have the ability to pro-actively manage this process by reviewing stock and placing orders with little management oversight. Less experienced purchasers will require management supervision of this process. Placing purchase orders is a serious process as it creates a binding legal financial obligation on the part of the purchasing entity. Sharing the purchasing and incoming order information with the sales team is very powerful in building sales and customer confidence for products that are not in stock. Higher levels of confidence typically drive higher profitability. Why does Fed-Ex charge three times as much as the U.S. Express mail system when the services are relatively the same 99% of the time? Consumer confidence is key!

Hopefully I have been able to accurately convey the importance of a well-run Purchasing Department, as well as the possible pitfalls we must avoid. Organizations that are committed to an efficient flow of communication and expectations will definitely reap the long-term benefits.

CHAPTER TWO:
WAREHOUSING & LOGISTICS

Entire books could be dedicated to this subject. I am by no means an expert within this field as my experience base is mostly with small to medium-size firms. The size of the organization will definitely impact the way companies address warehousing and logistics. My largest experience within this field entailed a 70,000 square foot facility with over 3,000 stock keeping units and 8 warehouse clerks that operated two shifts. This is relatively small compared to some of the macro-distribution centers that are managed by many of the big-box retailers and food wholesalers. Regardless of the size of the organization there are some points that I believe become universal to all. Most of them could be considered "common sense" observations, but I believe "common sense" is sometimes the least common of senses. Not only is common sense sometimes uncommon, but many times we forget to implement things that we know we should be doing, and we don't.

On three different occasions I have had an employee or colleague from large entities manage operations for my organization. One was from UPS; the other from Napa Auto Parts; and the third from BIC Corporation. All three of them had great experience working with large warehouse distribution and trucking systems with multiple warehouse locations and many stock keeping units (skus). All three of them agreed and encouraged the following concepts:

1. "In order to run a tight ship, you have to tighten the ship." The warehouse and logistics divisions should always be clean and organized. They should be run with a strong hand, and a no

nonsense type attitude. The rules and regulations should be clear so that safety and efficiency are guaranteed.

2. Warehousing and Logistics should help create a competitive advantage by doing the "common things uncommonly well". The team members should be aware that their functions are highly regarded within the organization. They should think of ways to receive, store, and ship products more efficiently. They should wonder, "How does my competition do my job?" and "How can I do it better than my competition?" Basically, "How can I be the best I can be?"

3. Hire excellent people! Train and motivate them by defining exactly how the warehouse and logistic functions impact the bottom line. Create measurement systems that will allow the individuals to improve upon.

4. Create simple systems and standards that do not require that your extraordinary individuals spend extraordinary efforts with simple processes. McDonalds® has been able to create one of the most successful fast food franchises using close to minimum wage individuals. Without a doubt these individuals should also be given the merit of accomplishment for what they are able to achieve. In addition to the individual's merit McDonalds has been able to help accomplish this by defining clear processes that are easy to follow.

Having the Operations and Logistics team understand the "customer service cycle" will help the team members better understand how the daily functions that they perform impact and benefit the entire organization. Imagine a very high end car dealership with a very beautiful showroom. The car brand has probably invested in a great deal of marketing tools in order to communicate their value proposition. They also have probably invested a lot of money in training their sales staff, as well as creating a "lifestyle" draw towards their brand. Imagine a customer who has been looking for their next vehicle for the last four months, comparing three different brands and models against one another. The customer finally makes up their mind and chooses the car they want. They spend a significant amount of money in the purchase or lease commitment. Imagine that when their new vehicle is delivered it is dirty. This almost never happens. Why? Delivering a dirty vehicle would defeat all the other previous positive customer experiences. The last thing the consumer would remember is receiving a dirty car. Car companies understand this process and have mastered the customer service cycle to ensure that the positive values are driven not only through delivery of the purchase but also later on with the maintenance of the vehicle. How many organizations understand this same concept? Can you think of organizations that complete their service cycle by including their operations and logistics teams? Can you think of organizations that do a great job at selling but a very poor job at delivery? Unfortunately there are many organizations that do not complete the cycle. They are missing out on opportunities to create better results long term.

CHAPTER THREE:

ACCOUNTING

Fortunately, good accounting has become a generally easy task for most organizations.

The profession has a continuous flow of bright and educated individuals, and the standards used are pretty universal. Additionally, good Information Systems help make the reporting process relatively easy. Despite all of these positive factors there are a couple of points to consider when trying to build an accounting team that is capable of helping create more value for the organization:

1. Hiring good people is once again crucial to having a team of accountants and bookkeepers that can add value to the organization. In order to achieve this you need to have a great leader. This will generally be your Controller, CFO, or Accounting Manager which will oversee the financial and reporting obligations of the organization. The leader should be dynamic and capable of understanding the core business indicators that drive profitability. He/She should be a connector that helps the CEO achieve unity and harmony within the organization while at the same time understanding the financial intricacies. The right leader will be capable of building a team that not only does accurate reporting, but is also made up of individuals who are personable enough to interact with other team members within the organization.

2. Timely reporting is crucial and should go without saying. Unfortunately many organizations do not receive their numbers on a timely basis. Some organizations do not use reporting as a

management tool. The financial reporting is the measuring stick which indicates if the business initiatives are working. Timely reporting allows the management team to make the proper adjustments that need tweaking.

3. Pay attention to your cash flow. I recommend always using a 13 week cash flow tool. Many software systems have them built in. When possible work with a "cash is king" mentality. Much of your cash philosophy will stem from the overall ownership expectations of return on investments. Cash crunches can obviously create great strife for organizations and need to be avoided at all cost. By the same token, the accounting team should stay away from over-reporting to avoid causing "analysis paralysis".

4. Utilize simple reporting systems and share key indicators with the appropriate team members that are responsible for the results. Share information sparingly without giving away the formulas of success to empower your team members to know how to impact the results.

CHAPTER FOUR:
HUMAN RESOURCES

Hopefully you have perceived the importance of Human Resources from the previous chapters. Employees are the most valuable asset that organizations have. Recruiting, hiring, and training should be crucial to the corporate objectives. When this process is managed well, organizations can achieve exponential growth. When Human Resources are managed poorly the results can be detrimental to the organization.

Not all organizations are large enough to have dedicated Human Resource departments. These organizations will have to rely on their individual managers to handle most of the functions. The CEO should be the top Human Resource developer with other HR professionals or managers working in tandem. Bradford D. Smart has written a very interesting book called Topgrading which deals with team development in a very aggressive way. His concepts work in practice. In the absence of HR professionals the top administrator, office manager, or Controller can help the CEO with leading the HR process. The top administrator also will oversee handling the bulk of the "paperwork" management used to generate payroll and tax compliance. No matter what the organizational structure, there are important Human Resource aspects that the department or management team should take into consideration:

1. Recruiting, hiring, and developing team members together compose one of the most important aspects of running an organization.

2. Take your time hiring the right individual and don't be afraid to pay for top performers. They will generate results.
3. 3. Quickly identify and re-circulate mediocre and poor performers into the marketplace.
4. Followthegoldenrule:"Do unto others what you would like to have done to you."
5. Make time to be face-to face with the team members. One of the common complaints that employees have regarding poor managers is their lack of accessibility.
6. Avoid negative interactions by focusing on positive improvements to behavior. Hire individuals you can trust rather than ones that have to be managed.
7. Understand employees wants, needs, and beliefs. Help them create and reach their goals.

CHAPTER FIVE:
OPERATIONS & ADMINSITRATION
CONCLUSION

Human beings are creatures of habit. Studies show that individuals personally replicate habits learned during the first nine years of life. Professional habits are usually learned within the first two years of experience. I have previously discussed the importance for top company leaders in defining clear visions and creating positive corporate culture. Make sure that these values and cultures are being transmitted and absorbed by the team members within their first two weeks at the organization. Make sure that the veteran members are given refreshers! It is important that this be achieved with all departments, but it is crucial to the development and contribution of the operational and administrative teams. These teams by the nature of their job requirements and surroundings are the anchors of the organization, while sales divisions tend to be more flexible and transient. It is not unusual to re-cycle sales individuals every 3-5 years while it is less typical to do the same with an A/P clerk or Traffic manager.

Make sure that the company leadership understands and appreciates the value of the operational and administrative team members. In so doing the individuals will respond by positively embracing the customer service cycle and help achieve the power of full engagement.

PART IV:
LEAD BY LISTENING AND
OBEYING CONCLUSION

"Congratulations! You have been promoted to CEO!"

Within the acknowledgements of this book I explained that many of the concepts developed within were inspired by Rosa Sugranes and Fernando Vila. The titles and principles were inspired by Rosa's father Ramon. In seeking inspiration for the conclusion I inevitably reached for the testimonies of Don Ramon captured by author Josep Ma. Tarragona in a book titled: <u>A Dream Achieved</u>. I read for a second time the sections that had to do with Ramon's history as well as those that pertained to Rosa, Fernando, and Marcelino. I couldn't help but smile as I read the excerpts and dawned on the realization of how powerful this wisdom has been over the years. To think of the amount of individuals that these concepts have impacted is flabbergasting to me. Ramon was the CEO of his organization from which was born Iberia Tiles with Rosa Sugranes as CEO. Fernando Vila married Rosa and left his professional accounting career to become CEO of Iberia Tiles and shortly thereafter Marcelino Sugranes became the CEO of the Spanish companies. Upon Fernando's assumption of his Iberia Tiles CEO role, Ramon told him that he would teach him how to become a businessman as long as he agreed to obey for two years. Fernando summarizes best as follows: "It is very simple, one can only lead if he or she knows how to obey. Youth now days do not really understand. They think that putting their knowledge to work is most important. To think that one is more intelligent than another could be true, but those whom think this are surely committing a mistake. The objective is not to know the right answers, but to be capable to analyze the situations and ask the right questions. The mistake young people make is to apply a known solution to the wrong situation. What is fundamental is to act with intelligence; towards what is beneficial to the organization. Many times, what is best for the business is not what one would like to implement. Here lies the great sacrifice of obedience."

Shortly after starting my career at Iberia Tiles, I was working a trade show whereby we had a booth open to public traffic at the Miami Convention Center. By 1994 Iberia Tiles had been around Miami for 15 years and was well known by most of the general public, and especially by a fair percentage of Cuban-American residents. During the trade show an elderly Cuban-American lady approached me for some product information. She approached me speaking Spanish (This is a very common behavior in Miami) and therefore I responded in my pure Castilian accent. After we finished our discourse, she asked if I was the owner of the business (apparently because she took note of my fluency with the language and because she knew that Iberia Tiles was from Spain). I quickly dispelled the idea and informed her that I was a mere employee. For some reason, I had the good fortune that Marcelino (Rosa's brother and Ramon's Son) was visiting from Spain and working the booth with me. After witnessing the encounter he quickly pulled me to the side and suggested that the next time I was asked that same question to respond affirmatively. He explained "All of us own Iberia Tiles. If not by stock, we own it by mere investment of time and return of investment via our payroll. Our customers like to purchase from individuals whom they feel have a vested interest in making sure their service or product is delivered correctly. The employees have the most vested interests in ensuring that the continuity and integrity of the organization is stable." From that day forward, I never again acted like an "employee" of Iberia Tiles. Ten years later I was fortunate enough to be able to become an equity owner at the same time I inherited the CEO duties from Fernando Vila. From that day forward, I promoted every single employee that I ever hired or trained to CEO. I obviously did not promote them officially to CEO by title as every ship must have one captain. I did although promote them to CEO in theory as I wanted them to confront all future situations as if they personally had the intellect, knowledge, and authority to personally deal with their responsibilities.

I also encourage you to become and act like the Chief Executive Officer of your organization. No matter your current role or situation, you are the CEO of your life and of your profession. God has given us the necessary tools for success. All we have to do is Lead, by Listening and Obeying.

www.ingramcontent.com/pod-product-compliance
Lightning Source LLC
Chambersburg PA
CBHW060533130626
46553CB00002B/732